SCHOLARSHIP
AND
SERVICE

SCHOLARSHIP
AND
SERVICE

THE POLICIES AND IDEALS OF A NATIONAL UNIVERSITY
IN A MODERN DEMOCRACY

BY

NICHOLAS MURRAY BUTLER

Essay Index Reprint Series

BOOKS FOR LIBRARIES PRESS
FREEPORT, NEW YORK

INTERNATIONAL STANDARD BOOK NUMBER:
0-8369-2220-4

LIBRARY OF CONGRESS CATALOG CARD NUMBER:
78-134066

PRINTED IN THE UNITED STATES OF AMERICA

TO THE TRUSTEES, FACULTIES, ALUMNI, AND
STUDENTS OF COLUMBIA UNIVERSITY, PAST AND
PRESENT, WHO HAVE HELPED TO BUILD A LIGHT-
HOUSE OF LEARNING TO THE END THAT NEW
GENERATIONS OF MEN MAY BE GUIDED TO KNOW
THE TRUTH WHICH SHALL MAKE THEM FREE

CONTENTS

INTRODUCTION

Of all institutions which modern man has built to give form and purpose to his civilization, the university is least understood. The law, the state, the church are eagerly discussed and disputed, but their meaning is a matter of general agreement. That the same may not be said of the university is due in large part to the university itself. The university has persisted in looking upon itself, and therefore has been largely looked upon, as merely an advanced type of school for the training of youth. In fact, however, the training of youth is a mere incident in the work of the modern university, which has been brought into being primarily to satisfy and to give body to the restless search of the human spirit for truth. It is the business of the university untiringly to seek for truth in all its forms, to hold fast to truth once gained, and to interpret it. The university in modern life represents, as did the cathedral in the Middle Ages, the noblest convictions and emotions of the human spirit. The cathedral was used as a place of religious worship to be sure, but its pointed arches, its pinnacles, and its majestic and harmonious beauty added to worship a physical expression of the noblest aspiration of those peoples who were then in the van of civilization. In like manner the university is certainly a place where youth are taught, but its existence, its many-sided activity, and its wide-spread influence give evidence of the purpose of mankind to make new conquests of the unknown and new uses of those conquests. The university that is not conscious of its real meaning and of the part which it may play in the history of the life of civilized man is a university in name only.

The papers that follow are an effort to interpret the modern university in terms of its ideals, of its problems, and of its counsels. Although the illustrations are drawn from the life of but one university, the principles which they make plain are common to all universities worthy of the name that seek to minister to the mind and the spirit of man, organized in his modern democratic society.

NICHOLAS MURRAY BUTLER

COLUMBIA UNIVERSITY
  IN THE CITY OF NEW YORK
  June 1, 1921

I

SCHOLARSHIP AND SERVICE

Inaugural address as twelfth president of Columbia University,
April 19, 1902

SCHOLARSHIP AND SERVICE

President Roosevelt, Mr. Chairman and gentlemen of the Trustees, my associates of the faculties, alumni and students of Columbia, our welcome guests, ladies and gentlemen:

For these kindly and generous greetings I am profoundly grateful. To make adequate response to them is beyond my power. The words that have been spoken humble as well as inspire. They express a confidence and a hopefulness which it will tax human capacity to the utmost to justify, while they picture a possible future for this university which fires the imagination and stirs the soul. We may truthfully say of Columbia, as Daniel Webster said of Massachusetts, that her past, at least, is secure; and we look into the future with high hope and happy augury.

To-day it would be pleasant to dwell upon the labors and the service of the splendid body of men and women, the university's teaching scholars, in whose keeping the honor and the glory of Columbia rest. Their learning, their devotion, and their skill call gratitude to the heart and words of praise to the lips. It would be pleasant, too, to think aloud of the procession of men which has gone out from Columbia's doors for well-nigh a century and a half to serve God and the state; and of those younger ones who are even

3

now lighting the lamps of their lives at the altar-fires of eternal truth. Equally pleasant would it be to pause to tell those who labor with us—north, south, east, and west—and our nation's schools, higher and lower alike, how much they have taught us and by what bonds of affection and fellow service we are linked to them.

All these themes crowd the mind as we reflect upon the significance of the ideals which we are gathered to celebrate; for this is no personal function. The passing of position or power from one servant of the university to another is but an incident; the university itself is lasting, let us hope eternal. Its spirit and its life, its usefulness and its service, are the proper subject for our contemplation to-day.

The shifting panorama of the centuries reveals three separate and underlying forces which shape and direct the higher civilization. Two of these have a spiritual character, and one appears to be, in part, at least, economic, although clearer vision may one day show that they all spring from a common source. These three forces are the church, the state, and science, or better, scholarship. Many have been their interdependences and manifold their intertwinings. Now one, now another seems uppermost. Charlemagne, Hildebrand, Darwin are central figures, each for his time. At one epoch these forces are in alliance, at another in opposition. Socrates died in prison, Bruno at the stake. Marcus Aurelius sat on an emperor's throne, and Thomas Aquinas ruled the mind of a universal church. All else is tributary to these three, and we grow in civilization as mankind comes to recognize the existence and the importance of each. It is commonplace that in the earliest family community church and state were one. The patriarch was both ruler and priest. There was neither division of labor nor separation of function. When development took place, church and state, while still substantially one, had distinct organs of expression. These often clashed, and the separation of the two principles was thereby hastened. As yet scholarship had hardly any representatives. When they did begin to appear, when science and philosophy took their rise, they were often prophets without honor either within or without their own country, and were either misunderstood or persecuted by church and state alike. But the time came when scholarship, truth-seeking for its own sake, had so far justified itself that both church and state united to give it permanent organization and a visible body. This organization and body was the university. For nearly ten centuries—a period longer than the history of parliamentary government or of Protestantism—the university has existed to embody the spirit of scholarship. Its arms have been extended to every science and to all letters. It has known periods of doubt, of weakness, and of obscurantism; but the spirit which gave it life has persisted and has overcome every obstacle. To-day, in the opening century, the university proudly asserts itself in every civilized land, not least in our own, as the bearer of a tradition and the servant of an ideal without which life would be barren, and the two remaining principles which underlie civilization robbed of half their power. To destroy the university would be to turn back the hands upon the dial of history for centuries; to cripple it is to put shackles upon every forward movement that we prize —research, industry, commerce, the liberal and practical arts and sciences. To support and enhance it is to set free new and vitalizing energy in every field of human endeavor. Scholarship has shown the world that knowledge is convertible into comfort, prosperity, and success, as well as into new and higher types of social order and of spirituality. "Take fast hold of instruction," said the Wise Man; "let her not go: keep her; for she is thy life."

Man's conception of what is most worth knowing and reflecting upon, of what may best compel his scholarly energies, has changed greatly with the years. His earliest impressions were of his own insignificance and of the stupendous powers and forces by which he was surrounded and ruled. The heavenly fires, the storm-cloud and the thunderbolt, the rush of waters and the change of seasons, all filled him with an awe which straightway saw in them manifestations of the superhuman and the divine. Man was absorbed in nature, a mythical and legendary nature to be sure, but still the nature out of which science was one day to arise. Then, at the call of Socrates, he turned his back on nature and sought to know himself; to learn the secrets of those mysterious and hidden processes by which he felt and thought and acted. The intellectual centre of gravity had passed from nature to man. From that day to this the goal of scholarship has been the understanding of both nature and man, the uniting of them in one scheme or plan of knowledge, and the explaining of them as the offspring of the omnipotent activity of a Creative Spirit, the Christian God. Slow and painful have been the steps toward the goal which to St. Augustine seemed so near at hand, but which has receded through the intervening centuries as the problems grew more complex and as the processes of inquiry became so refined that whole worlds of new and unsuspected facts revealed themselves. Scholars divided into two camps. The one would have ultimate and complete explanations at any cost; the other, overcome by the greatness of the undertaking, held that no explanation in a large or general way was possible. The one camp bred sciolism; the other narrow and helpless specialization.

At this point the modern university problem took its rise; and for over four hundred years the university has been striving to adjust its organization so that it may most effectively bend its energies to the solution of the problem as it is. For this purpose the university's scholars have unconsciously divided themselves into three types or classes: those who investigate and break new ground; those who explain, apply, and make understandable the fruits of new investigation; and those philosophically minded teachers who relate the new to the old, and, without dogma or intolerance, point to the lessons taught by the developing human spirit from its first blind gropings toward the light on the uplands of Asia or by the shores of the Mediterranean, through the insights of the world's great poets, artists, scientists, philosophers, statesmen, and priests, to its highly organized institutional and intellectual life of to-day. The purpose of scholarly activity requires for its accomplishment men of each of these three types. They are allies, not enemies; and happy the age, the people, or the university in which all three are well represented. It is for this reason that the university which does not strive to widen the boundaries of human knowledge, to tell the story of the new in terms that those familiar with the old can understand, and to put before its students a philosophical interpretation of historic civilization, is, I think, falling short of the demands which both society and university ideals themselves may fairly make.

A group of distinguished scholars in separate and narrow fields can no more constitute a university than a bundle of admirably developed nerves, without a brain and spinal cord, can produce all the activities of the human organism. It may be said, I think, of the unrelated and unexplained specialist, as Matthew Arnold said of the Puritan, that he is in great danger because he imagines himself in possession of a rule telling him the *unum necessarium*, or one thing needful; that he then remains satisfied with a very crude conception of what this rule really is, and what it tells him; and in this dangerous state of assurance and self-satisfaction proceeds to give full swing to a number of the instincts of his ordinary self. And these instincts, since he is but human, are toward a general view of the world from the very narrow and isolated spot on which he stands. Only the largest and bravest spirits can become great specialists in scholarship and resist this instinctive tendency to hasty and crude philosophizing. The true scholar is one who has been brought to see the full meaning of the words development and history. He must, in other words, be a free man as Aristotle understood the term. The free man is he who has a largeness of view which is unmistakable and which permits him to see the other side; a knowledge of the course of man's intellectual history and its meaning; a grasp of principles and a standard for judging them; the power and habit of reflection firmly established; a fine feeling for moral and intellectual distinctions; and the kindliness of spirit and nobility of purpose which are the support of genuine character. On this foundation highly specialized knowledge is scholarship; on a foundation of mere skill, deftness, or erudition it is not. The university is concerned with the promotion of the true scholarship. It asks it in its scholars who teach; it inculcates it in its scholars who learn. It believes that the languages, the literatures, the art, the science, and the institutions of those historic peoples who have successively occupied the centre of the stage on which the great human drama is being acted out are full of significance for the world of to-day; and it asks that those students who come to it to be led into special fields of inquiry, of professional study, or of practical application, shall have come to know something of all this in an earlier period of general and liberal studies.

Emerson's oration before the oldest American society of scholars, made nearly sixty-five years ago, is the magnetic pole toward which all other discussions of scholarship must inevitably point. His superb apology for scholarship and for the scholar as Man Thinking opened an era in our nation's intellectual life. The scholar, as Emerson drew him, is not oppressed by nature or averse from it, for he knows it as the opposite of his soul, answering to it part for part. He is not weighed down by books or by the views which Cicero, which Locke, which Bacon have given, for he knows that they were young men like himself when they wrote their books and gave their views. He is not a recluse or unfit for practical work, because he knows that every opportunity for action passed by is a loss of power. The scholar, in short, as the university views him and aims to conserve and to produce him and his type, is a free man, thinking and acting in the light of the world's knowledge and guided by its highest ideals.

In this sense the university is the organ of scholarship, and in this sense it aims to be its embodiment. The place of scholarship has been long since won and is more widely recognized and acknowledged than ever before. The church and the state which first gave it independence are in close alliance with it and it with them. The three are uniting in the effort to produce a reverent, well-ordered, and thoughtful democratic civilization in which the eternal standards of righteousness and truth will increasingly prevail.

But a university is not for scholarship alone. In these modern days the university is not apart from the activities of the world, but in them and of them. It deals with real problems and it relates itself to life as it is. The university is for both scholarship and service; and herein lies that ethical quality which makes the university a real person, bound by its very nature to the service of others. To fulfil its high calling the university must give and give freely to its students, to the world of learning and of scholarship, to the development of trade, commerce, and industry, to the community in which it has its home, and to the state and nation whose foster-child it is. A university's capacity for service is the rightful measure of its importunity. The university's service is to-day far greater, far more expensive, and in ways far more numerous than ever before. It has only lately learned to serve, and hence it has only lately learned the possibilities that lie open before it. Every legitimate demand for guidance, for leadership, for expert knowledge, for trained skill, for personal service, it is the bounden duty of the university to meet. It may not urge that it is too busy accumulating stores of learning and teaching students. Serve it must, as well as accumulate and teach, upon pain of loss of moral power and impairment of usefulness. At every call it must show that it is:

"Strong for service still, and unimpaired."

The time-old troubles of town and gown are relics of an academic aloofness which was never desirable and which is no longer possible.

In order to prepare itself for efficient service the university must count in its ranks men competent to be the intellectual and spiritual leaders of the nation and competent to train others for leadership. Great personalities make great universities. And great personalities must be left free to grow and express themselves, each in his own way, if they are to reach a maximum of efficiency.

Spiritual life is subject neither to mathematical rule nor to chemical analysis. Rational freedom is the goal toward which the human spirit moves, slowly but irresistibly, as the solar system toward a point in the constellation Hercules; and rational freedom is the best method for its movement. Moreover, different subjects in the field of knowledge and its applications require different approach and different treatment. It is the business of the university to foster each and all. It gives its powerful support to the learned professions, whose traditional number has of late been added to by architecture, engineering, and teaching, all of which are closely interwoven with the welfare of the community. It urges forward its investigators in every department, and rewards their achievements

with the academic laurel. It studies the conditions
under which school and college education may best be
given, and it takes active part in advancing them. In
particular, it guards the priceless treasure of that
liberal learning which I have described as underlying
all true scholarship, and gives to it full-hearted care
and protection. These are all acts of service direct
and powerful.

The university does still more. It lends its members
for expert and helpful service to nation, state, and
city. University men are rapidly mobilized for diplo-
matic service, for the negotiation of important treaties,
for the administration of dependencies, for special and
confidential service to the government, or some department of it, and, the task done, they return quietly to
the ranks of teaching scholars, as the soldiers in the
armies of the war between the States went back to
civil life without delay or friction. These same university men are found foremost in the ranks of good
citizenship everywhere and as laymen in the service of
the church. They carry hither and yon their practical
idealism, their disciplined minds, and their full information, and no human interest is without their
helpful and supporting strength. It is in ways like
these that the university has shown, a thousand times,
that sound theory and correct practice are two sides
of a shield. A theorist is one who sees, and the practical man must be in touch with theory if he is to see
what it is that he does.

What the future development of the great universities is to be perhaps no one can foresee. But this much is certain: Every city which, because of its size or wealth or position, aims to be a centre of enlightenment and a true world-capital must be the home of a great university. Here students and teachers will throng by the mere force of intellectual gravitation, and here service will abound from the mere host of opportunities. The city, not in its corporate capacity but as a spiritual entity, will be the main support of the university, and the university in turn will be the chief servant of the city's higher life. True citizens will vie with each other in strengthening the university for scholarship and for service. In doing so they can say, with Horace, that they have builded themselves monuments more lasting than bronze and loftier than the pyramids reared by kings, monuments which neither flood nor storm nor the long flight of years can overturn or destroy. Sir John de Balliol, doing a penance fixed by the abbot of Durham; Walter de Merton, making over his manor house and estates to secure to others the advantages which he had not himself enjoyed; John Harvard, leaving half his property and his library to the infant college by the Charles, and Elihu Yale, giving money and his books to the collegiate school in New Haven, have written their names on the roll of the immortals and have conferred untold benefits upon the human race. Who were their wealthy, powerful, and high-born contemporaries? Where are they in the grateful esteem of the generations that have come after them? What service have they made possible? What now avails their wealth, their power, their high birth? Balliol, Merton, Harvard, Yale are names known wherever the English language is spoken and beyond. They signify high purpose, zeal for learning, opposition to philistinism and ignorance. They are closely interwoven with the social, the religious, the political, the literary history of our race. Where else are there monuments such as theirs?

Scholarship and service are the true university's ideal. The university of to-day is not the "home of lost causes, and forsaken beliefs, and unpopular names, and impossible loyalties." It keeps step with the march of progress, widens its sympathies with growing knowledge, and among a democratic people seeks only to instruct, to uplift, and to serve, in order that the cause of religion and learning, and of human freedom and opportunity, may be continually advanced from century to century and from age to age.

II

FROM KING'S COLLEGE TO
COLUMBIA UNIVERSITY,
1754–1904

An oration in commemoration of the One Hundred and Fiftieth
Anniversary of the foundation of King's College, delivered at
Columbia University, October 31, 1904

FROM KING'S COLLEGE TO COLUMBIA
UNIVERSITY, 1754-1904

We are standing by one of the lines which imagination draws across the changeless chart of time. We
instinctively stop and look back. The mere flight of
time itself fills our minds with reverent wonder, and
we measure it off by decades and by centuries that
we may the better comprehend it. Yet it is not the
flight of time, but the story of accomplishment in
time—time's quality, may we say?—which instructs,
stimulates, and spurs us on. The record of the past
brings us knowledge of the subtle processes by which
ideas weave for themselves a material fabric. It counts
for us the steps by which man climbs the lofty heights
of his ideals.

What one hundred and fifty years of recorded time
is filled so full as the period of our university's life?
When before have the face of nature and the mind of
man both been so radically changed? The first president of King's College found the writings of Bacon and
of Newton to be novel and revolutionary. Stirred by
their teachings, he became, while still a tutor at Yale
College, the chief influence in displacing on these
shores the Ptolemaic conception of the universe for
the Copernican. From Ptolemy to Darwin, then, and
on to a world of divisible atoms and newly discovered

forces, stupendous but hidden, whose nature we only partially apprehend and comprehend not at all, so far it is from King's College to Columbia University.

A host of commonplaces of our modern thought were unknown to the generation which hailed the foundation of King's College. Newton had been dead but seventeen years, and his doctrines were as new and as startling to the rest of the world as they had been to President Samuel Johnson. Kant, who was destined to give its decisive character to modern philosophy, was but thirty years of age, and had not yet taken his university degree; perhaps no one outside of Königsberg had ever heard his name. Rousseau, the connecting-link between English revolutionary theory and French revolutionary practice, was in middle life and already becoming famous. Linnæus and Buffon were laying the foundations of a new natural history, but Lamarck, who was to reveal the modern theory of descent, was only a child of ten. Laplace at the tender age of five, and Lavoisier at eleven, could not yet be recognized as likely to make massive contributions to the sciences of mathematics and of chemistry. Of the publicists who were to guide the thought of English-speaking men at a great crisis, Burke was but six years out of Trinity College, Dublin, and had not yet entered Parliament; Washington was a youth of twenty-two, skirmishing with the French in what was then the Far West; Jefferson was a boy of eleven at play in Virginia, and Hamilton was unborn. The new university at Göttingen had been opened in 1737 with that liberty in teaching which was to build up the noble ideal of science as an end in itself that has since come to be the inspiration of every true scholar. But Halle and Göttingen, the first of modern universities, were wholly unknown in America, and Oxford and Cambridge were anything but safe models for the new college of the province of New York to follow. Dean Swift declared that he had heard persons of high rank say that they could learn nothing more at Oxford and Cambridge than to drink ale and smoke tobacco. Doctor Johnson found that when at Pembroke College he could attend lectures or stay away, as he liked, and that his gain was about the same either way. The poet Gray committed himself to the opinion that Cambridge must be the place once called Babylon, of which the prophet said the "wild beasts of the desert shall lie there; and their houses shall be full of doleful creatures; and owls shall dwell there, and satyrs shall dance there"; and "the forts and towers shall be for dens forever, a joy of wild asses." Just at this time Gibbon had completed the period of residence at Magdalen College which he afterward described as the most idle and unprofitable of his whole life. These harsh judgments are supported by the historian of Oxford, Warden Brodrick, who says explicitly that at this period the nation had lost confidence in Oxford education.

It was into a world of knowledge and thought totally different from ours that King's College was born a century and a half ago.

These provinces were remote in those days, and their settlers were chiefly bent upon material development and upbuilding. For the journey across the Atlantic to consume from four to six weeks was not unusual. Learning was of necessity at a low ebb, for the scholarly men who were among the first settlers had passed away, and their children and grandchildren, born in the colonies and reared there, had not much chance for a broad or a prolonged education. Harvard College had been in existence for a century and a quarter, and Yale for half a century, but both were hard pressed for means of subsistence, and their intellectual outlook was a contracted one. Jonathan Edwards had written, a few years earlier, that he took "very great content" from his instruction at Yale, and that the rest of the scholars did likewise. The College of New Jersey had recently begun instruction at Elizabethtown, and just as King's College opened its doors ground was breaking at Princeton for the first building of its permanent home. In Philadelphia Franklin was urging on the movement that was soon to give a college to that prosperous city, and throughout the colonies generally the need for a higher type of education was felt and efforts were making to supply it.

Then, as now, New York was often described as a city given over to trade and commerce to the neglect of higher and better things, but there is evidence that while the citizens were gaining the material substance with which to support a college, they were not neglectful of the fact that a college was sorely needed among them. For fully fifty years the idea of a college for the province of New York had been mooted, and general sentiment was favorable to it; but it was not until 1746 that the first step was taken to bring about the desired end. On December 6 of that year the legislature of the colony passed an act authorizing the raising of the sum of £250 by public lottery "for the advancement of learning and towards the founding of a college." The preamble of this act clearly shows that there was a wide-spread conviction that the welfare and reputation of the colony would be promoted by laying a proper and ample foundation for the regular education of youth. Other similar acts followed, and by 1752 nearly £3,500 had been raised by lottery for erecting a college. We smile now at the thought of supporting education through lotteries, but the practice was quite common in those days. Indeed, the lottery, which appears to have been a Florentine invention of some two hundred years earlier, had been invoked by Parliament the very year before that in which the charter of King's College was granted, in order to endow the British Museum. To purchase the Sloane collection, the Harleian manuscripts, and the Cottonian library, which collections formed the beginning of the British Museum, and to put the new institution upon its feet, the sum of £300,000 was authorized to be raised by public lottery.

The sum of £3,500, or thereabouts, raised by lottery for the college, was vested in trustees who were empowered to manage it, to accept additional contributions, and receive proposals from any city or county within the colony desirous of having the college erected therein. On May 20, 1754, these trustees, through William Livingston, one of their number, petitioned the lieutenant-governor, James De Lancey—the unhappy Governor Osborn having taken his own life, and no successor being yet appointed—to grant a charter of incorporation, either to them or to such other trustees as might be chosen, "the better to enable them to prosecute the said design of establishing a seminary or college for the instruction of youth." This petition also recited the fact that additional support had been found for the proposed college, in that "the Rector and inhabitants of the City of New York, in communion with the Church of England, as by law established, being willing to encourage the said good design of establishing a seminary or college for the education of youth in the liberal arts or sciences, have offered unto your petitioners a very valuable parcel of ground on the west side of Broadway, in the west ward of the City of New York, for the use of the said intended seminary or college, and are ready and desirous to convey the said lands for the said use, on condition that the head or master of the said seminary or college be a member of and in communion with the Church of England as by law established, and that the liturgy of the said church, or a collection of prayers out of the said liturgy, be the constant morning and evening service used in the said college forever." The petitioners obviously favored the acceptance of the conditions attached to the proposed grant, for they went on to say that they considered the site proposed to be "the most proper place for erecting the said seminary or college." This ground was part of the well-known King's Farm, which had evidently long been in mind as the site of the college of the province. For as early as 1703 the vestry of Trinity Church, before putting the farm out on lease, appointed the rector and churchwardens to wait upon Lord Cornbury, then governor, in order to learn what part of the farm he designed to use for the college which he (Cornbury) planned. It was March 5, 1752, when the vestry made the formal proposal to the commissioners appointed to receive proposals for the building of a college, and thereafter matters progressed speedily.

On October 31, 1754, James De Lancey, lieutenant-governor and commander-in-chief of the province of New York, signed the charter and attached thereto the great seal of the province. King's College "for the instruction and education of youth in the learned languages and liberal arts and sciences" was legally born. It is that act which we joyfully celebrate to-day.

It would not be profitable now to dwell upon the long and heated controversy that accompanied the foundation of the college. The seeds of the coming Revolution had already been sown, and in matters civil and ecclesiastical there were sharp differences of opinion among the colonists. On one hand it was felt that the conditions attached to the grant of land from Trinity Church were an unwarranted attempt to make

the new college of the province a sectarian institution, and that the charter should have come from the
assembly rather than from the king. In reply it was
urged that no conditions were thought of by Trinity
Church until ground had been given for the belief
that there was an intention to erect a college that
should have no religious associations whatever; and
that then only those conditions were imposed which,
liberally interpreted, would assure to the college a
Christian, but by no means a sectarian, relationship
and influence. The history of the college fully bears
out this view. As to the origin of the charter, it may
well be that the trustees of the original fund raised by
lottery, subsequently increased by a grant from the
excise moneys, were moved to petition the lieutenant-
governor rather than the assembly for a charter,
just because of the acrimony of the existing controversy and the fear of its results. However this may
be, the charter itself is a striking paper and one that
represents a point of view and a liberality of mind far
in advance of its time.

The charter makes express mention of the fact that
the college is founded not alone for the inhabitants of
the province of New York, but for those of all the
colonies and territories in America as well. Here, in
foresight and in prophecy, is the national university
that Columbia has since become. The charter assumes a public responsibility for the new college by
naming as trustees, *ex-officiis*, a number of representative public officials. Here, in foresight and in prophecy,

is the close relationship between the city and the college which has existed from that day to this, the more helpful in recent times because unofficial. The charter assures the liberality of the college in matters ecclesiastical and religious by designating as trustees, *ex-officiis*, the rector of Trinity Church, the senior minister of the Reformed Protestant Dutch Church, the minister of the ancient Lutheran Church, the minister of the French Church, and the minister of the Presbyterian congregation. The very next year the governors of the college united in a petition, which was granted, asking for power to establish a chair of divinity, the right to nomination for which should lie in the minister, elders, and deacons of the Reformed Protestant Dutch Church of the city. Here, in foresight and in prophecy, is that respect and regard for the Christian religion, and that catholicity of temper and tolerance of mind, which mark Columbia University of this later day. The charter expressly provides that no law or statute shall be made by the trustees which tends to exclude any person of any religious denomination whatever from equal liberty and advantage of education, or from any of the degrees, liberties, privileges, benefits, or immunities of the college on account of his particular tenets in matters of religion. Here, in foresight and in prophecy, is this splendid company of scholars and of students in which every part of the civilized world and every variety of religious faith are represented, all without prejudice.

This was a notable charter to be granted at a time

of bitter religious controversy and prevailing narrowness of vision, and the steps taken under it were worthy
of its far-reaching provisions. The presidency was
tendered to Samuel Johnson, one of the most remarkable men of his time; and it was he who gave to the
new college its educational form, its controlling tendencies, and its first ideals. Open-minded and catholic,
Doctor Johnson was the most scholarly American of
the period, and with Jonathan Edwards he takes rank
as one of the two really powerful and constructive
American philosophers of the eighteenth century.
Benjamin Franklin, who had been his publisher, consulted with him as to the plans for the projected college at Philadelphia, and urged him to become its head.
But Johnson was more strongly drawn toward New
York, in whose projects for a college he had long been
an interested counsellor, and for which his friend and
philosophical preceptor, Bishop Berkeley, had fed the
flame of his enthusiasm.

Doctor Johnson, sole lecturer, began instruction in
the month of July, 1754, some time before the charter
was granted, in the vestry-room of the schoolhouse
adjoining Trinity Church, of which the temporary use
had been allowed him. The requirements for admission to his first class were simple: the first five rules in
arithmetic, a knowledge of the Latin and Greek gram-
mars, and an ability to write grammatical Latin;
ability to read Cicero and the first books of the Æneid,
and some of the first chapters of the Gospel of St.
John in Greek. A warning was at the same time given

that higher qualifications would soon be exacted. Considering the state of opinion and the practice elsewhere, this declaration by President Johnson is remarkable: "That people may be better satisfied in sending their children for education to this college, it is to be understood that, as to religion, there is no intention to impose upon the scholars the peculiar tenets of any particular set of Christians, but to inculcate upon their tender minds the great principles of Christianity and morality in which true Christians of each denomination are generally agreed." So broad a tolerance as this is more usually associated with the end of the nineteenth century than with the middle of the eighteenth.

Moreover, this first president had a distinct vision of what was to follow from his small and modest beginnings; for he pictured the future in these words: "It is further the design of this College to instruct and perfect youth in the learned languages, and in the arts of reasoning exactly, of writing correctly and speaking eloquently, and in the arts of numbering and measuring, of surveying and navigation, of geography and history, of husbandry, commerce and government; and in the knowledge of all nature in the heavens above us, and in the air, water and earth around us, and in the various kinds of meteors, stones, mines and minerals, plants and animals, and of everything useful for the comfort, the convenience and the elegance of life in the chief manufactures; finally to lead them from the study of nature to the knowledge of themselves, and of the God of nature, their duty to him, themselves and one another." The felicity of phrase in this proclamation is not more remarkable than the clear recognition of the part to be played in education by the sciences of nature and their applications. Here spoke the mind stirred by the reading of Bacon and Newton, of Locke and Berkeley. The new science and the new philosophy were bearing their first-fruits here on this island, remote from the capitals of the world's affairs and far distant from the historic seats of the older learning.

On July 17 President Johnson, sole instructor, met his group of eight students. Bayard, Bloomer, Van Cortlandt, Cruger, Marston, Provoost, Ritzema, and Verplanck were the families represented on those slender benches. Good names all, some of them bearers of the sturdiest traditions of our city. Others followed, and it was not many years before the college roll was rich with the best names of old New York. There were Auchmuty, Barclay, Beekman, Bogert, Cutting, De Lancey, De Peyster, Griswold, Hoffman, Jay, Lispenard, Livingston, Morris, Nicholl, Pell, Philipse, Remsen, Romeyn, Roosevelt, Rutgers, Schuyler, Stevens, Townsend, Van Buren, and Watt—names which for generations have been in close and honorable association with the commerce, the society, and the politics of New York. Mr. Henry Adams is authority for the statements that before 1800 New York excelled New England in scientific work accomplished, and that New York was always an innovating influence. Study of the early history of our college and comparison of its professed aims and its outlook with those of the older institutions to the east and to the south justify his conclusions. And, slow as its development was in many ways, the history of Columbia College proves conclusively that it had always been an innovator and a leader. Its wise and far-sighted policies, more or less clearly formulated in detail, were for generations held back from execution only by lack of means. From the very beginning, though often with stumblings and delay, Columbia has trod the

> "Path to a clear-purposed goal,
> Path of advance!"

Our earlier teachers, like our later ones, were chosen for scholarship and character, wherever they were to be found. William Johnson, first tutor, came, as did his father, the president, from Yale. Leonard Cutting, who followed, was educated at Eton and Cambridge. Daniel Treadwell, first professor of mathematics, came, in 1757, from Harvard, and his successor, Harpur, from Glasgow. Myles Cooper was trained at Queen's College, Oxford, and Clossy, whose chair included the whole of natural science, at Trinity College, Dublin. Different view-points and varied associations helped make this company of early teachers cosmopolitan and open-minded.

The list of twelve presidents is unique in more than one respect. The two Johnsons and Barnard were graduates of Yale; Cooper came from Oxford; Wharton was trained at the English Jesuits' College of St. Omer, and was ordained a priest of the Roman Catholic Church; the first Moore held his degree from King's College, the second Moore and his two successors, now living, had theirs from Columbia; Harris was educated at Harvard; Duer at Winchester in the mother country and at Erasmus Hall on Long Island, and King at Harrow and Paris. The younger Johnson, who came to the presidency in 1787, was a layman, the first lay head of a college among English-speaking people of whom I find record; Duer, the second Moore, and King were also laymen, as was Barnard to all intents and purposes (though he took orders as an aid to his work in education and with no intention of engaging in parochial work), and as are the two presidents now living. Only Harris and Barnard died in office. The second Johnson and Duer were lawyers; the second Moore divided his energies between law and teaching; King was a merchant and editor, and Barnard was an educator in the fullest and highest sense of the word. Columbia, it will be seen, broke early with existing traditions, and the progressiveness and catholicity shown alike by the governing board and the teaching body were reflected in movements for educational advance that are as noteworthy as some of them are now seen to have been premature. The early and vigorous attention to the natural sciences under the lead of Clossy, Bard, Mitchill, and Hosack, the deep interest in public affairs and participation in them, which took the second Johnson to the

Constitutional Convention and then to the Senate of the United States, while still president, and Professor Mitchill to the legislature, to the House of Representatives, and to the Senate; the solicitous care for public education which spurred on De Witt Clinton, Henry Rutgers, and Peter A. Jay to lead the work of the Public School Society of the city of New York and so pave the way for the present municipal school system, were all prophetic of that zeal for scientific advance, for the public service, and for the education of the people which so strongly mark the Columbia of to-day.

Given so large a company of progressive men of science and of affairs, so noble a society of scholars, and so commanding a situation in this rapidly developing city, was not Columbia College unduly slow in reaching the plane of excellence and the wide scope of activity which were marked out for it from the very beginning? It certainly was, and the cause was grinding poverty.

The trustees of half a century ago had been facing problems which might well have staggered the bravest of them. It is more than twenty years since President Barnard, whose eager and far-sighted plans for Columbia were hemmed in on every side by lack of funds with which to carry them out, reviewed the financial history of the corporation and made it plain what the source of embarrassment and delay had been.

It is literally true that for a full century the college had to struggle for its life. The amount raised by lottery, increased somewhat by small legislative grants, appears to have been spent upon the first building and in the purchase of those materials that were necessary to the institution's work. The portion of the King's Farm granted by Trinity Church was valued at £4,000 or £5,000, but it lay beyond the limits of the inhabited portion of the island, and was for many years unproductive. It did, however, afford a commodious and convenient home for the college. The need for additional resources was early felt, and the royal governor of the province was appealed to for a grant of public land to the trustees. In response, a large tract of 24,000 acres, "comprising the township of Kingsland, in the County of Gloucester, in the Province of New York," was conveyed to the trustees by letters patent in 1770. Subsequently, however, in the settlement of the disputed boundary between New York and New Hampshire, this land, as well as 30,000 acres granted, in 1774, by Governor Tryon, was found to belong to what is now the State of Vermont, and it passed from the trustees without compensation. Gifts were few and small for many years, for the troubled times in the colonies were naturally not favorable to endowments for learning. Occasional legislative grants of small sums were rather an evidence of public interest in the college than serious attempts to upbuild it. Finally, in 1814, came the action which, through the courage and far-sightedness of the trustees, has meant so much to us. Upon a petition of the trustees setting forth that the extensive lands granted by earlier governors had been lost to the college, without compensation, in the settlement of the boundary dispute, the legislature granted to the college the so-called Hosack Botanic Garden, comprising the land in the city of New York now bounded by Fifth Avenue on the east, by Forty-seventh Street on the south, by Fifty-first Street on the north, and by a line distant about 100 feet from the easterly line of Sixth Avenue on the west, 260 city lots in all, then valued at $75,000. David Hosack, whose name this property bore and who had conveyed it to the State for a botanic garden, had been professor of botany in Columbia College from 1795 to 1811, and was a man of marked distinction in his day.

Therefore, the two historic endowments of the college which in these later days have become, through the growth and prosperity of the city, the main support of its rapidly expanding work, are gifts, the one from the church and the other from the state, to the upbuilding and defense of both of which the college has bent its every energy from the day of its foundation. In the King's Farm, or lower estate, and in the Hosack Botanic Garden, or upper estate, Columbia now holds tangible evidence of what religion and civil government have done for learning in this community, and it gratefully acknowledges its heavy obligation to them both.

But, splendid as the future of these properties was to be, they were not a source of immediate income. Quite the contrary; the cost of holding the property and of meeting the public charges upon it was an almost intolerable burden. In 1805 the income from the portion of the lower estate under lease was only about $1,400. Deficits faced the trustees with the closing of each annual account. Still they struggled on, having firm and clear faith in the future of the city and in the triumph of the high ideals committed to their keeping. The strong men who fought the fight during the long period of discouragement from 1810 to 1870—Rufus King and David B. Ogden, William Johnson and Beverly Robinson, Philip Hone and Samuel B. Ruggles, William Betts and Hamilton Fish, and their associates—they are those who saved this university for the twentieth century. It was 1863 before the slowly increasing income was sufficient to meet the cost of annual maintenance, and it was 1872 before the accumulated debt was wiped out. From that time begins a new chapter in the financial history of the corporation, a chapter which extends to the removal to the new home on Morningside Heights with its rapidly crowding opportunities and its heavy attendant responsibilities. It is plain, therefore, that the bare struggle for existence postponed almost to our own day that widening of influence and of scope, and that increase of activity, which had been part of the plan of the college from its earliest days.

"Debt," wrote President Barnard truly, "is no doubt a great evil, but there are evils worse than debt, and among these is stagnation." Columbia long bore the burden of debt and chafed in its heavy chains, but it is not true that it has ever been stagnant. At no time has it been without men whose scholarship and whose patriotic service in moulding the institutions and the public opinion of our young democracy, put them in the front rank of a university's heroes. The first Johnson was easily the most scholarly man in the colonies, and in philosophy a vigorous and progressive mind. The erudite Bard had no superior as a physician, and is gratefully remembered as sounding the call which brought into existence the Society of the New York Hospital. The second Johnson was fit companion to the noble company with whom he sat in the Constitutional Convention; it was he who proposed that the States should be equally represented, as States, in the Senate of the United States, and who, as chairman of the committee appointed to revise the style of the Constitution and arrange its articles, did much to give that instrument its familiar and admired form. With him in that noteworthy committee of five sat Alexander Hamilton of the Class of 1774 and Gouverneur Morris of the Class of 1768. Later, as senator from Connecticut while still president of the college, Johnson was a chief agent in framing the bill to organize the judiciary of the United States. Our own Hewitt has pointed out that it was De Witt Clinton, of 1786, who created the Erie Canal by which the wealth of the great West was opened up and poured into the lap of New York; that it was Robert R. Livingston, of 1765, who recognized the genius of Fulton and supplied the means to make steam navigation a success, and that it was John Stevens, of 1768, who

gave us the railway and the screw propeller, revolution-
izing transportation by land and sea. But for Livingston there would doubtless have been no Louisiana
Purchase, and our nation's history might have been
strangely different; and it was Mitchill who in the
legislative branch gave effective support to Jefferson's
plan to send Lewis and Clark across the undiscovered
mountains and to open for settlement the noble lands
"where rolls the Oregon." Kent, fit successor of
Bracton, Littleton, and Coke, not only taught students, but trained the public mind to an appreciation
of the fundamental concepts of American law. Mitchill, in his chair of natural history and chemistry,
was a fellow investigator with Lavoisier and Priestley,
and passing to the House of Representatives and to
the Senate, he was as serviceable to the state as to
science. Hosack was an influential figure in the early
development of botanical and medical science. Adrain,
a prince among mathematicians, preceded Gauss,
Laplace, and Herschel in his research concerning the
probabilities of error which happen in making obser-
vations. McVickar, versatile and powerful, was one
of the earliest American economists, the incumbent at
Columbia of the first chair of political economy of the
United States, and may fairly be claimed as the for-
mulator of the principles upon which our national
banking system rests. To Anderson and Davies mathematical teaching in America owes a debt which it is
glad to acknowledge, and it was Davies who, by his
text-books, familiarized American teachers and stu-

dents with the methods of exposition and study that had gained ground so largely in France. Anthon's copious stores of learning were freely drawn upon for the benefit of students of the Greek and Latin classics, and it was he who first made known in America the results of the vast researches chiefly by German scholars in the fields of classical history, philology, and archæology. Lieber's commanding figure and profound learning gave added weight to his luminous exposition of the philosophy of history. All these great men lived and served in the day of small things, and they have left splendid traditions and fortunate memories behind them. Not once in the long years of darkness and doubt, of difficulty and discouragement, was the college without commanding personalities among its governors and its teachers, or without worthy youths training for distinction on its scholars' benches.

From the day of its foundation our college was marked to become a great university. It had from its earliest beginnings no small or restricted conception of its mighty mission. It hailed its home in New York as a vantage-seat from which to influence the nation that lay behind and beyond. It was filled with plans for expansion and development that must have seemed strange enough to those who were content to plod along in the well-trodden path of the traditional college education of the day. From Doctor Johnson's first advertisement in 1754 to the academic legislation of most recent years, Columbia has had a university's ideals in view and has struggled earnestly toward their realization.

Instruction in divinity was planned as early as 1755, that in medicine was begun in 1763, and that in law in 1773. After the Revolution, when the name Columbia supplanted that of King's, the governors immediately voted to establish the four familiar university faculties of arts, medicine, law, and divinity. Hardly a decade has passed from that time to this when some ambitious spirit, either in the governing board or in the faculties, has not urged projects of expansion and advance. Most remarkable is the extraordinary scheme for a charter establishing "the American university in the province of New York," which was drafted at the express command of the governors of King's College, and which met with their formal approval on August 4, 1774. It contemplated a great institution composed of many parts, after the fashion of the French university organization completed by Napoleon. It was to confer any degree, and presumably, therefore, to give any instruction, given by any or all of the universities in England or Ireland. Read in the light of its date, the conception was an astounding one. This draft was transmitted to England and by command of the king was laid before him in council in April, 1775. With the record of that act the history of this remarkable document ends. Already the guns of Lexington and Concord were loading, and the urgent voices calling for the royal approval of the charter were drowned by the roar of the shot heard round the world. It may be permitted, however, to point out that no company of men given over solely to the pursuit of material well-being and the sordid accumulation of wealth could ever have entertained with sympathy and approval the noble conception of a great national university which that document revealed.

There are no worthier names upon our college roll than those of the men who from time to time urged projects of advancement and a wider growth. The report of 1784 was presented by a committee on which sat James Duane and Alexander Hamilton, John H. Livingston and Samuel Provoost, Nicholas Romaine and Morgan Lewis. The memorial of 1810 addressed to the legislature was drafted by Doctor Mason and urges that the trustees had been for some time "sedulously occupied in giving to the whole system of the college that improvement of which they are persuaded it is capable, and which when completed will elevate it to a rank that shall subserve the prosperity and redound to the honor of the State." This appeal was itself the result of a movement which had been begun two years earlier by the appointment of a committee of the strongest men on the board "to express their opinion generally as to the measures proper for carrying into full effect the design of this institution." Again in 1830 a far-reaching plan of expansion was adopted. When reported to the trustees it bore the signatures of Bishop Hobart, of Doctor Wainwright, of Doctor Onderdonk, of Doctor William Johnson, of John T. Irving, of Clement C. Moore, and of Charles King.

Once more, in 1852, at the instance of President King, another movement was begun to develop a university upon the foundation afforded by the old college. Long consideration was given to the ways and means to be adopted, and finally, in 1858, the elaborate plans that had been evolved were formally approved. William Betts, Henry James Anderson, Hamilton Fish, and Samuel B. Ruggles were those most largely concerned in their formulation. From that auspicious movement dates the beginning of the modern history of Columbia. No year has passed since the reports of 1854, 1857, and 1858 were submitted without some step forward being either planned or taken. It was under the impulse of this movement that the first university lectures were delivered; that the School of Law was definitely organized; that the College of Physicians and Surgeons was brought back to the university to occupy the traditional place of medicine therein, and that the School of Mines came into being to lead the way in this country in teaching the applications of modern science to a group of its great industries.

With the accession to the presidency of Barnard in 1864, there came to the service of the university one of the greatest figures, in many ways the greatest figure, in the whole history of our American education. His active and restless mind, which grew neither old nor tired, planned unceasingly and saw with astounding clearness of vision. Barnard is the greatest prophetic figure in the history of modern education. He first saw that the traditional college course was no longer adequate to meet the needs of modern youth; that it must be supplemented, extended, readjusted, and made more elastic, if it would serve under new conditions the same ends that it had served so well in the past. He exalted science and scientific research to their place of honor, and he swept with his keen vision the whole field of education and called upon the university to enter upon it as a subject of study and to treat teaching as a serious profession and not merely as an occupation. He gave his powerful influence to the movement for the opening of educational opportunities to women, and he felt keenly the limitations under which they suffered in his day. He looked out into new fields of inquiry and saw the significance of those studies in language, in archæology, in history and political science, in the physical and mathematical sciences, in experimental medicine, and in the science of life that are now gladly included in the wide circle of our university's care. What this generation has done Barnard planned and urged. Much of what remains for the next generation to accomplish he foresaw and exhibited.

One may be permitted to doubt whether, in the whole history of higher institutions of learning, there is another example of so consistent and steadfast pursuit of an ideal end as is shown in the history of the development from King's College to Columbia University. Broad scholarship, catholic sympathies, the widest scope, all have marked every plan proposed for adoption by the governing board. Even when it seemed impossible to sustain the academic life, men were planning not only to sustain it, but to enlarge and enrich it. Faith in this city and in this nation, faith in science and in philosophy, faith in public service and in lofty ideals has been the very life-blood of our college and university for the whole century and a half that has gone.

Twice in our history the pursuing city has driven us from our home. The King's Farm seemed far away from the centre of the small town of 1754. The Madison Avenue grounds were indisputably distant even from the resident section of 1857. But so rapid have been the strides of this metropolitan community that nothing less than the island's crown could suffice for Columbia's permanent need. Here, on soil where patriot strove and where nature reveals her beauty of rock and hill and stream, our university has made its permanent home with face bent upon a historic past, but eagerly expecting a historic future as well. No more will it seek to avoid a city's embrace, but set upon a hill where its light cannot be hid, it will be to the city as its very mind and soul. Commerce and finance will bring to New York physical strength and material wealth and hold high the symbols of commercial integrity. Transportation by land and sea and air will bring the travellers of the earth to our doors and seekers after knowledge from its remotest parts to these academic halls. The temples of religion will testify to our belief in God and his worship, and the

institutions of philanthropy to man's succoring hand
stretched out to his unfortunate fellow.   Above,
among, and about them will be the influence of our
university, preserving those things that should be preserved, discarding those things that are found to be
no longer true, and pursuing those things that are of
good report.   To this height shall come those impulses
of need which the city sends to call out our responding
service.   From this height shall go out those noble influences that will justify the struggles of the fathers
and the ample plans of those who have gone before.
Here in quiet and yet in activity, apart from the city
and yet in it, shall be the home of that grateful growth
from the early seed, a city's mind and a city's soul.

III

THE UNIVERSITY AND THE CITY

From the Annual Report as president of Columbia University,
October 6, 1902

THE UNIVERSITY AND THE CITY

The whole form of modern university development has been conditioned by the growth of great cities. The life of the modern universities is becoming more and more of the urban type. Each of the world's great capitals which is or aims to be a centre of influence in the largest sense of the word must and will be the home of a great university. That university will be national, or even international, in sympathy, scope, and influence. But it will be dependent in a large measure—when not, as in Europe, a governmental institution—upon the support of the city in which it is.

This university will of necessity reflect and extend the spirit and temper of that city. The drift of population into the great city centres is paralleled by the rapid growth of the number of students attending the city universities. While there is a difference of opinion as to the desirability of a city as a place of purely collegiate or undergraduate instruction, there is no doubt whatever as to the superiority of the city's opportunities and environment as a place of graduate, professional, and technical study. The history of Columbia College, which is the oldest part of Columbia University, and in a sense the mother of all the rest, shows clearly that during the past ten years at any rate an increasing number of parents in every part of the country are choosing New York and Columbia as a place to which to send their sons, even for the undergraduate period of study.

The reason for the vast and rapid development of the urban university is, as Cardinal Newman said two generations ago, that a city is by its very nature a university. It draws to itself men and women of all types and kinds, it is the home of great collections of art and science, and it affords abundant opportunities to come under the influence of the best music and the best literature of our time.

The great city, and especially New York, is intensely cosmopolitan, and contact with its life for a short time during the impressionableness of youth is in itself a liberal education. Columbia is the typical urban university, and in a sense the most national of all American institutions of higher learning. It typifies the earnestness, the strenuousness, the practicality, and the catholicity of New York City, and its constituency is drawn from every part of the nation. The tendency of American institutions once local to become truly national is a striking characteristic of the changes of the past quarter of a century. Perhaps no other American university has profited more than Columbia by the change, and perhaps none has done more to bring it about.

The universities at Paris, Berlin, Vienna, Munich, and New York owe their leadership to the fact that they are intent upon research and the training of productive scholars on the one hand, and upon the development and support of the highest possible professional training on the other. Each of these institutions is proud of the fact that its faculty includes a number of the unquestioned leaders in the world's science and the world's literature. It is the presence of men like these that constitutes a real university. And it is upon their influence and example that the university depends for its present and future usefulness.

The problems before Columbia University at the moment are twofold. The first is the problem which it has in common with all urban universities, namely, that of promoting productive scholarship and teaching efficiency. The second is the problem peculiar to a university which is situated in New York and which is, and aims to be, representative of all that is best in the traditions and ambitions of the American metropolis. This latter problem is, in fact, that of practical usefulness to the community and of effective leadership in all that concerns good citizenship and the highest personal and civic ideas. Columbia aims to keep always in close touch with the community of which it is so important a part. Its needs are enormous, but the capacity of New York to meet them is even greater; and we rely with confidence primarily upon the generous support and sympathy of the great city.

IV

THE SERVICE OF THE UNIVERSITY

Address at the dedication of the State Education Building at
Albany, New York, October 16, 1912

THE SERVICE OF THE UNIVERSITY

Mr. Chancellor, Regents, Mr. Commissioner, Ladies and Gentlemen:

The occasion that has brought together this distinguished and representative assemblage is no ordinary one. It has called from his post of duty across the sea the American ambassador to Great Britain in order that he may fill his distinguished place as chancellor of the University of the State of New York. It has summoned here representatives of public life, of education, and of institutions of learning from every part of our land, and from other lands as well; and it has called forth those messages of congratulation such as the commissioner has just read from the very edge of the world's latest war and from the capital city of one of the world's most heavily oppressed peoples.

It is an extraordinary occasion, and it is not to be passed by with a mere word of description of this great building, however noble, however magnificent, however monumental; because this building which we are here to dedicate to its high purpose in the presence of representatives of education of every form and type is itself the result of more than a century and a quarter of purposeful history. It puts into marble and stone and steel the visible embodiment of a great ideal.

The constructive spirit of Alexander Hamilton broods over this place. Whether or not Hamilton was himself the first to conceive of an American state system of education in which every educational interest and every type and form of instruction was to be included, makes very little difference. Whether Hamilton himself worked out the plan for the New York system of education, or whether he only aided and guided others in working it out, is a matter of no great present importance. Hamilton's philosophic insight, his broad vision, his practical capacity, are all represented and reflected in what this great building stands for and celebrates. That the framework of the educational system of the State of New York embodies the result of the conflicting views, political and social, of Alexander Hamilton and of George Clinton, we know. That the life history of that system bears in the fullest measure the evidence of Hamilton's genius and of Hamilton's intellectual vitality, is a matter of undisputed record and should be recalled on this day and in this presence.

The seed thought which underlies and gives purpose to the whole educational policy of New York from its very beginning—when it was a colony, when it was a province, and later when it became a State—is that the educational process is a unit and that its supervision and control should be gathered into one single department of state education. Rivalries, misunderstandings, personal interests, and ambitions long retarded the complete fulfilment of this fine aim. From the time of the first establishment in 1812 of the office of State Superintendent of Public Instruction until the enactment nearly ninety years later of the admirable law which is now in force and under which we live, the complete unification of the educational administration of the State proved to be impossible. That unification has now been wholly achieved. This building is its revelation and its embodiment. It has been achieved to the very great satisfaction, I feel sure, of every student of education and of the enlightened citizenship of the State. It is an achievement for New York; it is an example for our sister States.

This evidence of practical sagacity reflects and exemplifies a profound philosophic truth. The moment that we think straight about education and free ourselves from cant, from phrase-making, and from formulas, we know that intellectual and moral growth is an undivided process. We know that it cannot be divided into water-tight compartments, any one of which may be filled with ignorance while the human being affected still floats on the sea of intelligence. We know that it cannot be cut up into fragments at war among themselves, with some one fragment taking precedence over others. We know that every educational institution has a common purpose and a common end, and that to attempt to set one against the other, to bring about conflict and rivalry and jealousy between them, is to incite educational civil war. The division of education into stages, the classification of educational institutions into types, is a mere matter of administrative convenience, a simple administrative device with nothing to justify it but our administrative convenience and necessity. If any one supposes that this device rests upon some profound principle that fixes a gulf between one stage or grade of education and another, and that compels these stages to have different and disputing interests, then in my judgment that person is absolutely wrong. It is a constant struggle in all of our educational administration to keep these administrative conveniences in the subordinate place where they belong. We are always to have a great and serious care that our administrative devices are not erected into shibboleths and so made the means of cramping, narrowing, or crushing the life history of even a single human soul.

The point of this remark lies, as an American humorist has said, in the application of it. That application is this: The process which this building symbolizes, the process to aid and guide which the school, the college, and the university are founded, is one that would go on in some fashion if schools and colleges and universities had never been heard of. These institutions do not create education, although they sometimes conspire to make it extremely difficult. When one reflects upon the ravages which have been committed in the name of education and upon the assaults on our intelligence which have been made by educated men, he sees the point of view of the cynic who would urge us to agitate for compulsory illiteracy! He is disposed to paraphrase the dying words of Madame Roland, and to cry out: "Oh, education, what crimes are committed in thy name!" All of which means that our supreme care in reflecting upon this great public interest must be to keep it natural, to keep it true, to keep it free from contamination alike by false and low ideals and by mere mechanical devices.

Education suffers sometimes from those who rush to aid it, from those who invent mechanical devices for it and who become so much more interested in the mechanical device than in the process itself. If we could only learn that all our devices, all our machinery, are subordinate and adjuvant, and are to be kept in their proper place! When we become supremely wise and supremely skilful perhaps we shall be able to dispense with them altogether.

At the heart of this educational process, giving it great dignity and direction, lies the most precious thing in the world, human personality. Human personality is an end in itself. To watch it grow, to help it grow, to take note of the results of its growth are a constant joy and delight. The putting forth of new power, the giving evidence of a capacity previously non-existent, and the growing responsibility for capable and wise self-direction are the tests of an education that is real rather than one that is merely formal and mechanical.

This human personality begins to manifest itself at birth, and already in the kindergarten and in the elementary school it is the subject of observation and care; but it is precisely this same human personality, a little more mature, a little better disciplined, a little more closely addicted to fixed habits, that gives purpose to the university. There is no qualitative change; there is a quantitative gain in power, in habit, in capacity; but the quality, the essence, the spiritual life at the seat and centre of the process are precisely the same at whatever point in the institutional scale you bring it under observation.

The responsibility of the university is doubly great because of its traditions, because of its resources, because of its equipment, because of its opportunity, and because it is the last of man's formal expressions of method as to the proper training of his fellow man. The university is the very last rung on the trellis-work that we put up in order that this tender plant, reaching up from earth toward heaven, may find something upon which to rest its tendrils as it grows out into an independent strength and life of its own. But the university cannot be out of sympathy or out of contact with the schools, with the institutions of every type that deal with human personality in its earlier and less mature forms. A true university is a proving-ground for personality and for intellectual power and a splendid gymnasium for the exercise of the muscles of the intellect and of the will. The primary purpose of the university is to provide the companionship of scholars for scholars at a time when sufficient maturity has been reached to make the joy of the intellectual life intense and productive. If I may borrow a charming phrase from a colleague of mine, I should say that a university is a company of scholars in which those who have discovered the mind make full, profitable, and productive use of their discovery.

The temptation to define a university is very great and the task is very difficult. The university has manifested itself in many forms and in many ways. It is a far cry from the little group of students of the art of healing who gathered long ago about a bubbling spring in the south of Italy and made the University of Salerno; from the band of eager scholars of the Roman law who congregated in Bologna to hear Irnerius tell what it was that the Roman world, already lost, had left in form and structure to the civilization that the barbarian peoples were building upon the place where Rome once was; from the day when a band of these students exposed themselves to heat, to cold, to fatigue, to expense, to danger, in order that they might tramp, foot weary, across the plains of France to hear the masters of the schools expound the knowledge of the time on the hills that rise on either side of the River Seine, which were the birthplace of the University of Paris—it is a far cry, I say, from all that to the great busy universities of Berlin, of Vienna, of Paris, to the halls and walls of Oxford and of Cambridge, to Edinburgh and to St. Andrews, to the universities of our own land, of Canada, and those on the other shore of the southern sea. But they all have something in common. It is possible to seek and to find that common denominator and to relate all these great undertakings and achievements of the human spirit in a class and so to define them.

Nearly twenty years ago I ventured to offer a definition of a university which I have seen no reason to change. A college of the liberal arts is not a university, even if its requirements for admission be higher or more complicated than usual. The college has its task, which is the training of American citizens who shall be educated gentlemen. A college surrounded by or allied to a group of technical or professional faculties or schools is not a university. A university is an institution where students adequately trained by previous study of the liberal arts and sciences are led into special fields of learning and research by teachers of high excellence and originality, and where by the agency of libraries, museums, laboratories, and publications knowledge is conserved, advanced, and disseminated. Teaching is only one function of a university, and perhaps the smallest one. Its chief function is the conservation, the advancement, and the dissemination of knowledge, the pushing out of that border-line between the known and the unknown which constitutes the human horizon. The student who has felt the thrill of discovery, however slight, however unimportant; the student who has put his foot on ground in letters, in science, in philosophy, where no man's foot had ever been before, knows what it is to feel the exaltation of discovery. He has entered into the spirit of the university. He has joined the household of Socrates.

What the Germans call the philosophical faculty is at once the essence and the glory of the university.

There can be no university where the spirit and the methods of this faculty do not dominate. Indeed, a university is a thing, a place, a spirit, and not a name at all. No institution can become a university by merely calling itself so. It must come into spiritual kinship with those that have worthily borne the name since universities were. If Mr. Lowell exaggerated a little when he said at Harvard some years ago that a university is a place where nothing useful is taught, surely he exaggerated on the right side. Doubtless what he had in mind was the fact that the university is a place where everything else is not subordinated to the immediately gainful or practical. The university is the resting-place of those activities, those scholarly aspirations, those intellectual endeavors which make for spiritual insight, spiritual depth, and spiritual beauty, but which cannot be transmuted into any coin less base than highest human service.

Then the university relates itself in closest fashion to the needs and aspirations of the state, the civic order, the community. The university is the home of that freedom of the spirit which is liberty; liberty to think, liberty to speak, liberty to teach, always observing those limits which common sense, right feeling, and a decent respect for the opinions of mankind put upon all of us.

It has seemed to me that man's faith in liberty has weakened a good deal in these later years. As I read the signs of the times abroad and at home, I should say that man's belief in liberty is less vital, his grip upon it less firm, than they were a hundred years ago. On every side and in almost every land it is now proposed to achieve those aims for which liberty has been supposed to be the best agent, by substituting for liberty the essentially mediæval instrument of regulation. There are strong and able men who believe that what the single tyrant could not accomplish the many-headed majority may do. It appears to be likely that the world will undergo another experience of this time-old experiment which has been tried so often, until once more its futility is made plain to every one; and then, doubtless after some of us are gone, by common consent the search for liberty and its right exercise will be resumed.

But there is happily no sign that liberty is to be driven out of the university. If the universities give liberty a home and keep alive the little flame that has illumined the world so brightly and so long, man is just as sure to return to the pursuit of liberty and its right exercise as the dawn is to follow the darkest night.

Liberty implies a discipline which is self-discipline, and liberty is not license. It implies a discipline by which the human spirit has taken over from the world about it, from history, from tradition, from morality, from human feeling, a great fund of material and made it into habits of self-control, self-direction, self-ordering. The institutions of civilization are the world's highest and best example of a disciplined liberty. It is a function of the university to show liberty at work under the restraint which self-discipline imposes,

Moreover, true liberty implies reverence and carries reverence in its breast; reverence for that which lasts, reverence for that which has proved itself, reverence for that which bears the marks of excellence, reverence for that which calls man up out of and above himself. That university falls short of its opportunity which does not give constant lessons in a liberty that is self-disciplined and that is reverent.

This liberty which the university cherishes is the persistent foe of all forms of artificial equality, of all forms of mechanical procedure, and of all manifestations of a smug satisfaction with chains of an intellectual and moral narrowness. It is a function of the university in every land to make this so plain that he who runs may read.

We must not shut our eyes to the fact that the task of the university grows greater as the difficulties of democracy grow heavier and more numerous. But the university dare not shrink from its responsibility, from its call to public service, from its protection of liberty. The university must not follow, it must lead. The university must not seek for popularity, it must remain true to principle. The university must not sacrifice its independence either through fear of criticism or abuse or through hope of favors and of gain. We dare not be false to our great tradition. Remember that of all existing institutions of civilization which have had their origin in the western world, the university is now the oldest save only the Christian church and the Roman law. The university has witnessed the decline and fall of empires, the migration of peoples, the discovery of continents, and one revolution after another in the intellectual, social, and political life of man. Of all these the university may say, in the well-known words of the pious Æneas, omitting only his adjective of misery,

> "Quæque ipse vidi
> Et quorum pars magna fui."

The university has been at the heart and centre of almost every great movement in the western world that has an intellectual aspect or an intellectual origin. Its responsibility was never so heavy as it is to-day. This is true whether you look to Germany, to Italy, to France, to Russia, to England, to Scotland, to Canada, to America, to the Latin-American republics, or to the new commonwealths of Australia and South Africa. What is it that the statesmen of New China, feeling the flow of a fresh life-blood in the nation's veins, first propose to imitate out of all the world? They wish to imitate the university as Europe and America know it, and for the very purposes which have made it so permanent and so powerful in Europe and in America.

We are looking out, by common consent, upon a new and changing intellectual and social sea. The sight is unfamiliar to the individual but not to the university. The university has seen it so often, whether the change has been for good or for ill, that the university knows that if only it keeps its mind clear and its heart true and the prow of its ship turned toward the pole-star, it will survive these changes, whatever they may be, and will contribute to make them beneficent. The university knows by long experience that it will come out of all these changes stronger, more influential, and bearing a heavier responsibility than ever.

I do not speak of the university which is brick and stone and mortar and steel. I do not even speak of the university which is books and laboratories and classrooms and thronging companies of students. I speak of the university as a great human ideal. I speak of it as the free pursuit of truth by scholars in association, partly for the joy of discovery in the pursuit of knowledge, partly for the service to one's fellow men through the results of discovery and the pursuit of knowledge.

When I look back and remember what the university so conceived has done, when I remember the great names, the noble characters, the splendid achievements that are built forever into its thousand and more years of history, I think I can see that we have only to remain true to our high tradition, only to hold fast to our inflexible purpose, only to continue to nourish a disciplined and reverent liberty, to make it certain that the university will remain to serve mankind when even the marble and steel of this great building will have crumbled and rusted into dust.

V

MEMORY AND FAITH

Address at the Annual Commemoration Service, St. Paul's Chapel,
Columbia University, December 6, 1914

MEMORY AND FAITH

To one who knows and loves Columbia University and who has passed his whole life in the university's service, this day and this occasion are full of solemn significance. In our noble commemoration service we are to reflect on the immortality of the university, its ideals, its hopes, its achievements on the one hand, and on the quick passing of even the fullest and the longest human life on the other. The occasion invites us to compare these two phenomena and to interpret them each in terms of the other. We are to picture to ourselves for a few moments the planning and the upbuilding of one of humanity's freest and finest products, and we are to dwell upon the life and the services of those workmen whose task on the great structure is done. To some it was given to draw plans and to lay foundations; to others it was given to aid wisely and well in making the superstructure rise upward through the long course of years; to still others it was given to add to the building those marks of beauty which are the fruit of genius and to surround it with those tender associations which are the accompaniment of fine and gentle character. Where the task is infinite and the time unending there can be no appraisal of service in terms of accomplishment. The greatest accomplishment seems small indeed when measured by such standards. Service in such a task must be appraised, recorded, and lovingly dwelt upon n terms of sacrifice, of purpose, of spirit.

The progress of civilization—if civilization has really progressed—is marked in each of its several stages by typical visible institutions into which the prophets, the seers, and the spiritual leaders of an epoch put all that is best in themselves and in their time. The spiritual life, the reflection, and the aspiration of the Middle Ages poured themselves out into those great cathedrals which dot the hills and plains of Europe, with their towers and spires pointing toward the heaven that they fain would reach, with their windows bearing in superb adornment symbolic representation of all that the Middle Ages held most dear, and with their doors wide open that all men might enter to see and hear and share in their message and in their meaning. The form of reflection and the form of faith that built those splendid churches are no longer found dominant among us, but they themselves remain, not alone as monuments of one of the most splendid periods in the whole record of human achievement but as milestones along the pathway of the human spirit toward its distant goal. Even to-day we can almost see the patient artist of centuries long gone working with devoted skill and with loving care to the end that an arch, a window, an altar-piece, or a pinnacle might be made more beautiful and might carry forever on its carved face more of what he himself, in his simple-minded, placid faith, was and felt. Time has passed; stupendous changes have come over the mind and the spirit of man, and another form of human institution has pushed the cathedral aside into history. That newer institution is almost as old as the cathedral itself, but it was ages long in coming into its full inheritance. That institution is the university. Everywhere the university embodies the ambitions, the ideals, and the hopes of the age in which we live. It includes the anxious and assiduous pursuit of truth on the one hand, and the training and guiding of the younger generation on the other, as well as the pouring out of all the fruits of its experience and its wisdom before the people so that the whole people may share those fruits to their inestimable advantage.

He who really understands a university and enters into its spirit understands his own time and all time. The university puts behind it and away from it the meaner and the baser motives and feelings. It has no place for greed, for jealousy, for vanity, or for empty boasting. The only emulation it admits is emulation in the pursuit of truth and in the service of mankind. Its life is an open book; its treasures are the men who make it and the men whom it in turn makes. No other product of humanity—no form of government, no work of letters or of art, no discovery in science, and no new conquest of nature's forces— is so human, so truly human, and so fully representative of humanity as is the university truly conceived. Its fabric may be bombarded and burnt, but its spirit cannot be touched by cannon or by fire. It may be deprived of means with which to exert its powers and capacities to the utmost, but it cannot be prevented from doing all that is possible for it to do in pursuit of its everlasting and uplifting purpose. Those who can see in the university nothing more than a group of stately buildings, a collection of rare and useful books, quantities of modern and well-adapted apparatus, and thronging companies of students eager to be shown how to grasp hold of life in some fashion that will produce adequate economic return, do not see the university at all. All these things are there, but they are on the surface only. The deeper things in a university's life and history are only known and felt by those who are able to go beneath the surface as it presents itself day by day, and to feel the majestic onward sweep of the great current of spiritual life with its grand tradition that finds in the university at once a garment and a form of highest and most lasting expression.

It is from a university so conceived that there have gone out in the year now closing many noble and generous lives. Some of them had been so fortunate as to be permitted to carry large and heavy stones to the rising structure and to leave their names carved forever upon it. Others have been mysteriously taken from the work when life was all before them, when they were just beginning to feel the joy of the task and to appreciate in some measure its larger meanings. To-day we remember them not alone for what they did, but for what they wished to do; and we like to believe that somewhere and somehow beyond this ken

of ours they are able to go forward unfettered with
their work.

Philosophers and poets have in turn been moved to
look upon life now as a tragedy and now as a comedy.
For one it is an inexplicable mystery, and for another
it is something that can be in every part weighed,
measured, counted, and in so far understood. In fact,
life is all these things and yet none of them. It has
an aspect, as it turns its face to the revolving sun of
time, that is now tragic, now comic, now mysterious,
now understandable; but it is much more than all
these and far different from them all. Life is so much
the ultimate fact that everything else must be stated
in terms of it, while it can be adequately stated in
terms of nothing but itself. The serene penetration of
a Sophocles, the robust aspiration of a St. Augustine,
the subtle gentleness of a Pascal, and the magical reflective power of a Kant have all been exhausted, and
more than exhausted, in attempting to transmute life
into language and life's problems into simpler terms.
Sophocles, St. Augustine, Pascal, and Kant have become immortal through the literally splendid character of their studies and portrayals of life; but life
remains after all that they and a thousand others have
contributed to its understanding, the ultimate fact.
Its absence is as inconceivable as its extinction is incredible.

In this commemoration service we stand in contemplation of the two most impressive and controlling
facts of life—memory and faith. It is upon memory
and upon faith that we rest for everything that we

call real and for everything that we call inspiring. Odd as it may sound, there is no such thing as the present. By the present we mean only the invisible dividing line between what has just been and what will in an instant be. While we speak the little word now with which we try to fix the passing moment, that moment has already gone to join the unmeasured and the unplumbed past which looks to memory alone for its existence. The intuition of Heraclitus was correct. Everything constantly changes. What we really mean by the present is the most recently past, with perhaps some reference to the nearer aspects of the oncoming future. What is past is in turn drawn by the slender and imperceptible thread of the present from the exhaustless store of that future which is posited by faith and on which that same faith builds all of life's activities, hopes, and ambitions. We remember those who were with us on yesterday and we have faith that they will be with us again on the morrow. He who would build his life only upon what he sees and hears and touches, and therefore upon what he thinks he knows, builds not upon reality but upon the oldest and most persistent of illusions. The philosophical egotist, heedless of the teaching of Socrates, hath said in his heart that there is no world but his own. Upon him we need waste no words, but may leave him in self-satisfied contemplation of his petty product.

To-day, then, we find ourselves first of all remembering. We recall with affection the names, the forms, the activities of those who are no longer within our sight. They are very real and ever present to us by reason of our manifold and powerful associations with them. We can trace their footsteps and the marks of their handiwork in, about, and upon the fabric, seen and unseen, of the university of our love. Then we turn from our memory to our faith. We try in vain to picture where those who have gone may now be or how they may now be at work. Somehow we cannot divest ourselves of the feeling, the belief, the faith that, while there has been interruption in the form of their activity and in the conditions of their existence, that activity and that existence still are. The alternative revolts intelligence and reduces reason to irrationality.

There is yet another figure which helps us to link our memory and our faith. In this university we have before our eyes one of the storied hanging-gardens of the world. Into it there come each year hundreds, and even thousands, of tender shoots of the human plant. In this garden they are set out, sometimes in even rows, sometimes irregularly, according as each one will flourish best. They are nourished and cared for. They are trained to grow upward, and, if it be their nature, they are made to stand alone and to support their own weight. In the fulness of time these tender shoots have grown into fine strong plants and trees. They put forth buds and flowers. They throw protecting shade, and when the due time comes they ripen and scatter themselves over the soil of the garden to enrich and to fertilize it for new generations like their own. They have manifested their

presence and they have left a remembrance, some of
beauty, some of strength, some of protecting shade,
some of fertilizing and enriching power. Each one
has done its part. Each has drawn into itself from
the soil of the garden in which it is set, rich with the
tradition and human service of over a century and a
half, and from the atmosphere of freedom and confident hope that glistens round about, those foods which
each living thing knows how to choose and to make
into structure, and, through structure, to grow, to
blossom, to fade, and to pass back into the great
stream of life from which all life comes. In this hang-
ing-garden there is no death. There is only that
changed life which brings forth life again more abundantly.

> "I with uncovered head
> Salute the sacred dead,
> Who went, and who return not.—Say not so!
> 'Tis not the grapes of Canaan that repay,
> But the high faith that failed not by the way;
> Virtue treads paths that end not in the grave;
> No bar of endless night exiles the brave;
>
> .　.　.　.　.　.　.　.
>
> In every nobler mood
> We feel the orient of their spirit glow,
> Part of our life's unalterable good,
> Of all our saintlier aspiration;
> They come transfigured back,
> Secure from change in their high-hearted ways,
> Beautiful evermore, and with the rays
> Of morn on their white Shields of Expectation!"

VI

THE UNIVERSITY PRESIDENT, UNIVERSITY TEACHER, AND UNIVERSITY STUDENT

Address at Johns Hopkins University on Commemoration Day,
February 22, 1915

THE UNIVERSITY PRESIDENT, UNIVERSITY TEACHER, AND UNIVERSITY STUDENT

In accordance with fortunate custom, members of this university are assembled to commemorate its ideals and its purposes, to recall with affectionate regard the names of those great ornaments of the university who are gone, and on this occasion also to wish Godspeed to him who has recently been chosen to its high office of president.

More or less that is not new has of late been written about this office, as well as more or less that is not true. The office itself is in its historic evolution the outgrowth and the product of personality. It depends for its usefulness and effectiveness wholly upon personality and not at all upon authority. Judged by the length and the security of tenure of its various incumbents at different institutions, the office is what would be called in the business world an extra-hazardous risk. Disturbance relating to it is not infrequent, and eviction from it is not unknown. Nevertheless, ambition to hold it is well-nigh universal among academic persons.

The beginnings of the modern office of university president are to be seen in the careers of Tappan at Michigan, of Wayland at Brown, and of Anderson at Rochester. Barnard, of Mississippi and of Columbia, was probably the first to give to the office its significant relationship to general educational policy and to the philosophy of education. White of Cornell, Gilman of Johns Hopkins, and Harper of Chicago were the earliest of that small but powerful group who have been able to put their hands to the invigorating and inspiring task of creating a new institution out of an idea. Eliot of Harvard is the pioneer among those whose work and pleasure it has been to put a wholly new and reconstructed modern building upon an old and highly respected foundation. These men, two of whom fortunately still live to give us constant counsel and guidance, will occupy the chief places in our academic Pantheon of the nineteenth century. As their names are heard it will be recognized that they have, each in his own way, helped to establish another striking characteristic of the office that they adorned— its direct relation to public service and to the instruction and elevation of public opinion. It is a matter of just pride to those who have chosen the academic life and who follow it, that American citizenship and American scholarship bear upon their rolls such names as these.

It is worth while to notice the reaching out in other lands, where universities are much older than with us and where tradition is less rudely disturbed than is so often the case here, for the establishment among them of those academic relationships and responsibilities that have done such service in America. When the Ministerialdirektor in the Cultusministerium of Prus-

sia is a sufficiently powerful personality, he is in effect
president not of one Prussian university but of the entire eleven. Shortly before his death I was walking
one summer day in the forest at Wilhelmshöhe with
Doctor Friedrich Althoff, a true ἀναξ ἀνδρῶν and one
of the most devoted and efficient administrators of
education that the world has known. Doctor Althoff
was then, and had been for many years, Ministerialdirektor in the Prussian Cultusministerium. He asked
a number of questions as to how university business
was transacted in America, as to how responsibility for
certain acts and policies was fixed, and in particular as
to how appointments to important academic posts
were made. When in reply the great variety of methods for doing all these things in the United States was
described to him at some length, Doctor Althoff threw
up his hands in despair and said: "Impracticable!
Impossible! Here I do all that myself, or take care
that it is done." He went on to express the hope that
his life might be spared to work out some plan for the
better organization of the Prussian universities to the
end that, without in any way separating them from the
ultimate and complete control of the state, each university might have an administrative head of its own
charged with substantially the same duties as fall to
the lot of a university president in America. In France
the accomplished Liard in Paris, and in Great Britain
the principals of the four Scottish universities, as well
as Michael Sadler at Leeds, Herbert Fisher at Shef-
field, and Sir Henry Miers, just now leaving London

for Manchester, have duties and responsibilities that are in most respects analogous to those that devolve upon the university president here. Upon the judicious and far-sighted use of the opportunities that the office affords will depend in large measure the influence, the importance, and the productiveness of the universities of the world during the next generation or two.

The duties and responsibilities of the office of university president may be summed up in very few words. They are the jealous care and close oversight of the work and interests of the university taken as a whole, and the guidance of its relations toward the public. The statutes of a given university may be more or less specific in regard to the office of the president, and they may intrust to the incumbent of that office greater or less authority, but the fact remains that the office will be in chief part what the incumbent makes it, and the measure of its authority will be the force of his personality. No autocrat and no self-seeker can long maintain himself in it. A great office makes a great man seem greater still by reason of the opportunity it affords him for the use of his powers; a great office makes a small man seem smaller still by reason of the fierce light which it causes to fall upon his littleness. It is one of the most satisfactory incidents in the history of the American democracy that it has brought into existence an important and conspicuous office whose incumbent is set apart by his very incumbency to represent in our American life the principles and ideals upon which universities are built and for which they exist, and to hold these principles and these ideals insistently before the public attention. The man of letters, the experimental scientist, the accomplished student of history or of economics, is, by reason of his university position, under obligation to represent one aspect of university activity and university interest to the public at large. It is the function of the university president to represent the university and that for which it stands in their entirety. In any large and complex university organization the wise president will live almost entirely in the future. The detailed matters of to-day will be dealt with by others. He, however, will constantly scan the horizon on the outlook for new problems and new opportunities for scholarship and for service.

Within the university itself it is the proper function of the president to be the friend and counsellor both of the scholars who teach and of the scholars who learn. He has the opportunity and privilege to bring to the consideration of their several problems and difficulties the point of view of the whole university, and thereby to place at the service of each individual teacher and student who seeks his aid the results of consideration given elsewhere to similar problems and of experience in dealing with them that others have had. It is also his duty to interpret the plans, the policies, and the needs of the university's teachers and directors of research to such governing body as may exist to hold and to care for the university's property and to allot its income in aid of various university undertakings.

All this was clearly understood and admirably stated by President Gilman when he wrote at the very beginnings of this university these words concerning the office of the president:

The President of the University is the authorized means of communication between the Board and the various officers of instruction and administration employed in the University; it shall be his duty to consult with the Professors in respect to the development of their various departments, and the general interests of the University; to determine the appropriate duties of the Associates and Fellows; and to exercise such superintendence over the buildings, apparatus, books and other property as will ensure their protection and appropriate use. In respect to these matters and all others which concern the welfare of the University, he shall consult frequently with the Executive Committee, and he shall attend the meetings of the Board of Trustees. Purchases, alterations, repairs, and other incidental expenses must not be ordered by any of the officers of the University without his previous assent or the expressed authority of the Board.

Nothing would be more unfortunate than for the office of university president to cease to be an educational post and to become merely a business occupation. Such a change would certainly be followed by the speedy deterioration of the university's ideals and by the unconscious commercialization of its methods. With such a change the reign of the questionnaire— wretched word!—would be abroad in the land, and the ubiquitous inquisitor, governmental or private, armed with his measuring-rod, his tape line, and his tables of statistics, would speedily reduce the university to a not very desirable form of factory. Systems of cost-accounting would displace productive scholarship in furnishing a standard of judgment as to a university's management and usefulness.

The notion that appears to be held by some that there is a divergence of interest between those teachers who teach and those teachers who are chosen to have particular responsibility for the care and support of teaching is wholly illusory. It is the true function of educational administration to reduce machinery to a minimum, to keep it out of sight and as much as possible out of mind, and as completely as means will permit to set free the two great and largely interdependent functions of teaching and research.

At no time has the academic career been so important as it is to-day, at no time has it ever been so well compensated, and at no time have those who pursue it been offered larger opportunities for the exercise of influence on public opinion. It is now the custom everywhere in the world to seek the counsel and the opinion of the professorial class when any matter of public interest is under consideration or in dispute. This applies, unfortunately, not only to matters of which the professorial class have cognizance, but also to matters of which they know little or nothing. The result has been to put a new and strange burden upon professors and to offer a temptation to the assumption of infallibility that has proved too much for some academic persons in more lands than one. The performances, both vocal and other, of not a few university professors in many countries, including our own, in connection with the great war in Europe, have made it seem desirable to many of us to insist upon dropping the title of Professor and to substitute for it the less combative Mister.

It is the fashion of the moment not to have any fixed principles of knowledge or of conduct, but to profess belief in the capacity and ability of each individual to make a world philosophy of his own out of such materials as chance and temperament may provide. This fashion is quite closely followed just now by large numbers of those in academic life, and indeed it is sometimes exalted as the one sure and certain method of finding an acceptable substitute for truth. There would appear to be need of a new Socrates who, whether as gadfly or in some less disagreeable guise, shall do over again what some of us had supposed was satisfactorily done once for all during the closing decades of the stirring fifth century before Christ. It is a long time since Socrates extracted from Gorgias the admission that with the ignorant the ignorant man is more persuasive than he who has knowledge.

One result of so many differing man-made, or professor-made, universities is a frequency and variety of conflict that it would tax the mathematician to enumerate and the historian to classify. The notion that nothing much that is permanent and worth while has been either known or accomplished until our own brave selves came upon the scene makes education difficult and, from some points of view, impossible. If the world is to begin over again whenever a new appointment is made to a professorial chair, it is reasonably plain that the man in the street will soon dispense with the services and the guidance of the men of everlasting beginnings. In much the same way we are now asked to believe that whenever a callow youth makes a minute addition to his own stock of information the sum total of human knowledge has been increased as the result of scientific investigation. It is just this mixing up of the individual with the cosmos and of the morning paper with the history of civilization that is the weakest point in academic teaching at the present time, particularly in those subjects which once were history, economics, politics, ethics, and public law. Those who remember the striking lectures of Heinrich von Treitschke, recently discovered by England and America and now much discussed in both countries, will recall the fact that he gave but scant attention to the teaching of the history of Europe and of Germany, although his chair was supposed to deal with those subjects. What Von Treitschke really did was to make lectures on the history of Europe and of Germany the vehicle for the very effective and emphatic expression of his own personal opinions on men and things in the world about him. In some degree, therefore, Von Treitschke was the forerunner of that now very considerable class of American university professors who devote no small part of their time to expressing to their students their own personal views on the politics, the literature, and the society of the day, while in form offering instruction on anything from astronomy to zoology. There is something to be said for the policy of making academic teaching effective by relating it to present-day interests and problems, but there is nothing to be said for turning academic teaching into an exercise in contemporary journalism. When every considerable town has its own Napoleon of finance and every political group its Hamilton or its Jefferson, there is some danger of getting mixed as to standards.

All these are troubles which have come upon the professorial class as a result of the public appeal made to us for an expression of opinion on current topics. If one be a profound student of Plato he is expected without warning to pass an illuminating critical judgment upon the latest outgiving of Mr. George Bernard Shaw. If he happens to be well versed in the economic thought of Germany and Austria, he is called upon for an authoritative expression of opinion regarding the strike of coal-miners in Colorado. If by any chance he has ever written a book on any aspect of railway organization, management, or finance, he runs the risk of being clapped upon a public commission to supervise and in part to control the railway systems of a state or nation. All these are dangers and embarrassments to which the alert university professor, whose name is known in the newspaper offices, is now constantly subjected. Avoidance of them is possible only for the sagacious and well-balanced scholar who knows that no single master-key will unlock all human doors of difficulty.

One of the chief tools of the present-day academic conjurer is the blessed word sociology, particularly in the hands of some one not a trained sociologist. Both Auguste Comte and Herbert Spencer would be not a little surprised to see what has become of the term that they fondled so tenderly. It is now stretched to include everything that can possibly relate to the diagnosis of social ills as well as everything that can possibly relate to social therapeutics. Not even the subtlest of physicists has yet worked out a theory of the elasticity of gases that is adequate to explain the potentialities of the word sociology. This word, once so innocent and so impressive, is now under a cloud because of its attempt to establish a world-empire. Poetry and alchemy, science and song, religion and mythology, philosophy and magic, are all reduced to mere counters in its great world-game. Naturally these smaller and ambitious states have become restless and are showing signs of revolt. They wish to be permitted to live their own lives and not to be made mere vassals of a mighty overlord who possesses all knowledge, who wields all power, and who monopolizes all explanations. Just now law is under attack from a curious mixture of sentiment and lore that calls itself sociological jurisprudence, and which I understand to be a sort of legal osteopathy. We can only await with some concern the reactions in the appropriate laboratories when a sociological physics, a sociological chemistry, and a sociological anatomy appear upon the scene.

Of the American university student it must be said that in far too many instances he is prevented from getting on as well as he should because he is over-taught. In particular, he is overlectured. The traditions of school and college are still strong in the universities, and the ideal university relations of scholarly companionship between teacher and taught have difficulty in establishing and in maintaining themselves. To use—or rather to abuse—the academic lecture by making it a medium for the conveyance of mere information is to shut one's eyes to the fact that the art of printing has been discovered. The proper use of the lecture is the critical interpretation by the older scholar of the information which the younger scholar has gained for himself. Its object is to inspire and to guide and by no means merely to inform.

Indeed, there is some reason to doubt whether the undue dominance and prominence of the didactic point of view in the modern university is altogether an advantage. The happy days at Bologna when the students and their rector managed the university, when professorial punctuality was enforced by fines, and when the familiar professorial practice of dwelling unduly on the earlier parts of a subject to the neglect of the later parts was checked by the expedient of dividing a topic into *puncta* and requiring the doctor to reach each *punctum* by a specified date, certainly had much to commend them. Then it was the students who made the rules and disciplined their teachers; now it is the teachers who make the rules and discipline their students.

The chief object of the university's teaching, of its libraries and its laboratories, is after all to arouse intellectual interest, to stimulate curiosity, and to send out a young man on his voyage of discovery filled with ardent enthusiasm, enriched by close association with wise and noble-hearted men, and imbued with the high ambition to make the most of himself and of his chosen field of study. If even the most numerously attended university can do this for a hundred men each year, and if five of the hundred become distinguished and one of the five eminent, that university has been successful. It has done a noteworthy service to American life, to scholarship, and to science.

VII

THE AMERICAN COLLEGE

Address delivered at Swarthmore College, November 14, 1902

THE AMERICAN COLLEGE

Somewhere in the neighborhood of 1820 the American college, as the term is traditionally used and popularly understood, came into existence. Before 1820 it would be difficult to distinguish the college, except perhaps in two or three instances, from the secondary school of familiar form to-day, the high school or academy. This college uniformly (so far as I know) gave a four-year course of instruction in prescribed studies. The students came at the age of fifteen or sixteen and were graduated at nineteen or twenty. They were disciplined carefully in a narrow intellectual field, and it did most of them great good. They were obliged to do many things they did not like in ways not of their own choosing, and they gained in strength and fibre of character thereby. Ambitious boys who looked forward to law or theology, and often to medicine too, as a professional career, sought the college training and college association as a basis and groundwork for their later studies and their active careers. For the most part they acquitted themselves well, and the sort of training that the college gave commended itself to the intelligent people of the country. The nation was young and crude in those days, and it was pushing far out into new and unbroken territory. It had rivers to bridge, forests to hew, fields to clear and to sow, homes to build, States to found. That was a noble era of creative industry. Life was often hard and luxuries were few. Yet the college went wherever the population broke a way for it. Eleven colleges were founded before the Revolution, and 12 between 1783 and 1800; no fewer than 33 came into existence during the thirty years that followed, and 180 between 1830 and the close of the Civil War. Many of those founded before 1830 were in the newly broken territory. Two were in western Pennsylvania, 5 in Ohio, 3 in Kentucky, 1 in Tennessee, 1 in Indiana, 3 in Illinois, and 1 in Missouri. These colleges differed from each other in many ways, but they agreed in that they conferred one degree at the conclusion of the course, that of bachelor of arts, for substantially the same kind and amount of work. Postgraduate studies, so called, were almost or quite unknown, and the completion of a college course was the attainment of a liberal education, as the phrase goes. Judged by to-day's rigorous and exacting standards of scholarship, the graduates of these colleges did not know very much. Nevertheless, their minds were carefully trained by devoted teachers, sometimes men of rare genius and human insight, and they loved letters for their own sake. They grew in manhood and came out of the college halls full of ardor in the pursuit of high ideals.

It was this sort of institution which gave the American college its reputation and which put into the degree of A. B. the valued significance which it has now so largely lost. Latin, Greek, and mathematics were the only subjects a knowledge of which was required for entrance to this college. The Latin included grammar, four books of Cæsar's *Commentaries,* six books of Vergil's *Æneid,* and six orations of Cicero. The Greek included grammar, three books of Xenophon's *Anabasis,* and two of Homer's *Iliad.* The mathematics included arithmetic, a portion of plane geometry, and algebra as far as quadratic equations. These subjects the boy mastered in school or academy or by private tuition; everything else that he learned was in the college course. Many of the weaker and less fortunate colleges gave some, or even nearly all, of this instruction themselves.

The college course, properly so called, was made up of more Latin, Greek, and mathematics, some English literature and rhetoric, a little logic, a little political economy, a little moral philosophy, and, usually, a little mental philosophy or metaphysics. Occasionally chemistry crept in; more often a combination of mechanics and physics called natural philosophy. History, unless it was ancient history, played a small part, and the modern European languages were rarely included.

This institution, with the requirements for admission that I have named, with the course of study that I have outlined, the students being (usually) from sixteen to twenty years of age, is the college which distinguishes the American educational system from that of Europe. The degree that it gave is the A. B. degree of the golden age to which one hears such continual harking back. What has become of this institution, the American college?

The college, or academical department, embedded in the great universities of to-day, is the lineal descendant of the old college, but strangely unlike its ancestor. Even the separate and independent college—the small college, as it is called—is in many ways very different from the older institution of the same name. The changes and improvements of the past fifty years have removed many of the old educational landmarks and rearranged many of the old elements of secondary and collegiate instruction. To speak to-day in the terms of fifty years ago, without marking carefully the changes in the meaning of those terms, is to talk nonsense.

Almost the only colleges which retain the characteristics of the old, traditional type are those which have been without the means to respond favorably to the influences which have destroyed that type. The small college with low standards of admission to a four-year course is closer to the American college of history and of rhetoric than is any other.

But if the old college itself has disappeared, the ideal for which it stood remains. That ideal was to train men roundly, thoroughly, and well for manly and worthy living. Their spirits were to be furnished, not their pockets filled, by a course of study and training which fell just at the right period of their lives, and by close and intimate association with others having aims similar to their own. No purpose could be more lofty than this, none more practical among a democratic people.

What the old college used to do in four years to this end is now done in part by the new college and in part by the secondary school. Four years are still required to complete the traditional course of study in the liberal arts and sciences, but the whole four years are no longer passed under one institutional roof. Taking Columbia College as a standard, one half of the old college's work, measured in terms both of time and of content, is done by the secondary school and the results are tested by the college admission examination. This change has come about by the general raising of the requirements for admission, both in quantity and in quality, which has gone on at most colleges since 1860. These requirements for admission have been raised because the country has been better served by having the earlier part of the work formerly done in college transferred to the secondary schools. So transferred this work has been brought within the reach of tens of thousands of boys who could never have left home to get it, and who could never have entered upon a four-year college course for lack of means. In 1898 only one third of the nearly twenty thousand boys who were graduated from the public high schools looked forward to a course in a college or a scientific school, and only 7.18 per cent of all the boys in the public high schools were preparing for a college course of the old type. If they had had to depend upon the college alone for their liberal studies, they would have known nothing of them. Moreover, secondary-school teaching nowadays compares very favorably with college teaching. The best secondary schools have scholarly teachers, well-furnished libraries, and well-equipped laboratories that many a college might well envy. Some of the newer subjects are, on the whole, taught better in the high schools than in many colleges.

These are my reasons for believing that the change which has raised the requirements for admission to college is a good one and a permanent one.

While this change has been taking place, the colleges have for the most part drifted. Too few of them have followed clearly conceived and persistently executed policies. Most of them have been simply played upon by forces from without, and these forces have been received with varying degrees of stubbornness. Hence the chaos of standards and of degrees which exists at this moment. Where the requirements for admission have been raised since 1860 by two years of work and where the course of study in college is still four years long, there is a six-year course in the liberal arts and sciences in the place of the old four-year course. Where the requirements for admission have been raised, and the years spent in college lessened by one, there is a five-year course in the liberal arts and sciences in place of the old four-year course. Where the requirements for admission have been raised and a four-year course in college maintained, one or two years of which are given to professional studies, there is left a four-year or a five-year course (as the case may be) in the liberal arts and sciences, and the degree of A. B. is no longer given wholly for work in arts, but for work partly in arts and partly in professional studies. In some cases the phrase liberal arts and sciences is interpreted broadly, in some narrowly. Often an attempt is made to distinguish between the older group of college studies and the newer ones, and degrees of bachelor of letters, science, and philosophy have been introduced to mark the completion of the courses other than the traditional one.

Some or all of these changes and developments may be decided improvements upon the older order of things, but the point I wish to make is that the results are not colleges or college courses as those words were once used. Discussions of the new in terms of the old are futile and misleading unless the terms employed are carefully distinguished and defined. In current discussions and debates about the place and value of the college there is easily noticeable a good deal of unconscious juggling with words and an equally noticeable lack of acquaintance with the facts as they are. It is a perfectly defensible position to hold that even with the raised requirements for admission the college course should still be four years in length, but this position must not be defended by appeals to the old college and its standards. The supporter of this position is not a conservative; he is a radical innovator who holds that a six-year course is now necessary in order to lay the basis for professional studies and to make the preparation for life for which four years formerly sufficed. He must defend his new plan and must prove that it promotes scholarship, strengthens character, and increases the influence and the usefulness of the college in our democratic society. If he can do these things I, for one, will throw in my lot with him without hesitation. If he cannot prove his case, then I prefer to pursue the old ideal along established lines by methods adapted to our new knowledge and our wider experience.

As I view the facts, the traditional American college is disappearing before our eyes, and will, unless the disintegrating influences are checked, disappear entirely in another generation or two. What we shall have left will be either an agreeable finishing school, or country club, for the sons of the well-to-do, or a combination of academy and school of general science. This, again, may be a good thing; and it may, on the whole, be a gain rather than a loss to assimilate our educational system to those of continental Europe by eliminating the college as the connecting-link between secondary school and university. But those who so hold must not argue in the name of the college which they would destroy. They must defend the early specialization involved in putting—or rather in keeping—the professional and technical schools right on top of the secondary school. They must defend the transformation of the American college into a university faculty of philosophy. It is because I do not believe that either defense can be successful that I differ with those who attempt these things, and prefer to make a struggle to retain the American college as such.

The two most active and dangerous foes of the American college to-day appear to me to be those who regard a secondary-school training as adequate preparation for professional and technical study in a university, and those who, mistaking the form for the substance, insist that the course of collegiate study must be four years or nothing, unless it be that an especially hardworking student is permitted to squeeze four years' work into three.

The former sacrifice the ideal to the commercial and the material, and make every school of law, medicine, divinity, and technology in the land a competitor of the college. The college cannot stand that sort of competition indefinitely, and our life will be the poorer and the narrower if it goes.

The latter, by transforming the college into a university, at least for the latter half of its course, not only radically alter the college training and the college degree considered as ends in themselves, but also put the college in a position where it is economically impossible and, from the view-point of social service and educational effectiveness, unwise to require the completion of its course as a prerequisite to professional and technical study. In only four professional schools has this been done, two schools of law and two schools of medicine; and already, I am told, expressions of dissatisfaction, or incomplete satisfaction, with the result are heard. The fact that the policy is indefensible is clearly shown by the tendency to permit so-called college students to pursue professional studies for one or two years of the undergraduate course. This is an elaborate evasion of the issue, and one by which the degree of A. B. is made either meaningless as an arts degree or else one given for the completion of a two or a three year course in the liberal arts and sciences, and not for one of four years.

Again I say that these new conditions may conceivably be better than those which they displace. But, if so, the American college is gone and in its place has come a new and different institution, no matter what its name, and the baccalaureate degree is hereafter to be a university and not a college degree. It seems to me to be perfectly clear that in this case the small college will eventually disappear utterly, even though the name survives. The collegiate or academical department of a university will continue in a position of increasing insignificance—save where maintained for a longer or a shorter time by special causes—as an American shadow of a German faculty of philosophy.

Probably few or none of us wish for any such development as this. Least of all is it wished for by those who insist so strongly upon the maintenance, at all hazards, of a four-year college course and the existing standards of admission; yet it is the almost certain result of the policy which they are now pressing upon us. Mistaking words for things, they are striking heavy blows at that which they would like to protect. They should realize the force of the statement of Francis

Wayland, even truer now than when made sixty years ago: "There is nothing magical or imperative in the term of four years, nor has it any natural relation to a course of study. It was adopted as a matter of accident; and can have, of itself, no important bearing on the subject in hand."

I want to retain the college not alone as the vestibule to the university where scholars are trained and where men master the elements of the professional knowledge required in the practice of law, medicine, teaching, engineering, and other similar callings, but as the school wherein men are made ready for the work of life. If the college is wisely guided these next twenty-five years, its students who are looking forward to active business careers after graduation ought far to exceed in number those who choose scholarship or a learned profession as a career. For such students the college will be all in all; and with no university course or professional school to look forward to, the college will be the one centre of their academic memories and affections. But to draw such students and to hold them in large numbers, and so to impress itself upon the country as effectively in the future as in the past, the college must be really a college and leave off trying to be a university. This means that it must come back into its own natural and most useful place.

Plans to bring this about have been proposed. Most of them aim at shortening the time devoted to the course of the new college, and so at getting rid of one or two of the extra years that have been put on to the course in liberal arts and sciences since 1860. The reasons why any lowering of the standard of admission to college would be against the public interest, I have already stated. Three different plans of getting through with the college course in three years instead of in four have been suggested. The first is to reduce the amount of work required for the degree so that it can be readily completed in three years. This is the plan at Harvard College, where the twenty-one courses required for the A. B. degree in 1880 have been displaced by a requirement of seventeen and one-half courses, one and one-half of which may be anticipated at entrance. The second is to permit a student to take four years' work in three, if physically and mentally competent to do so. This plan seems to me objectionable, in that it throws upon the student rather than upon the college the necessity of meeting a new and involved educational situation. It also tempts some men to overwork, others to loaf.

The third plan, and the one which commends itself to my judgment, is to recast and remodel the college course entirely on a two-year or a three-year basis according to the standard set—and upheld—for admission. The existing four-year course cannot be squeezed and pulled into a two-year or a three-year shape. It cannot be offered to one student on one set of conditions and to others on another set. There must be an entire reconstruction, and the new course, whether it occupy two years or three, must have a unity, a proportion, and a definiteness of its own. It must be a pyramid with a new altitude, and not the old pyramid truncated. It must be built of the best of the old bricks with plenty of new ones added thereto.

It should be borne in mind, too, that, contrary to the hypothesis of some critics, the new and shortened college course is not at all the result of the widely prevalent tendency to hurry or to "hustle," nor is it suggested only by the needs of the professional schools in the great universities. It will, I think, displace the longer course because it is intellectually, ethically, and educationally better. It will train better men and render greater public service than will the present spun-out four-year course with its inclusion of almost every subject of study known to man. There is no more obvious psychological fallacy than to suppose that the longer the time spent in getting an education, the better the results. The chances are that the contrary is true. Habits of dawdling, drifting, and incomplete and unconcentrated attention persisted in from sixteen or eighteen to twenty or twenty-two years of age will weaken any but the very strongest minds and characters. Less time better used is a useful motto for the colleges to adopt.

In the reconstruction which is just beginning, in the effort to get back the American college and to keep it, much depends upon enforcing a sound and helpful standard for admission to college. This has been, and in many cases is yet, the most difficult part of the problem to deal with. But the progress of the past few years is astonishing and full of promise. Co-operation between colleges and between colleges and schools has given us the College Entrance Examination Board, whose uplifting and steadying influence is felt everywhere. Through it the secondary schools learn what to aim at, and the colleges learn what to expect and insist upon. The enormous educational advantages of an examination are gained, while the difficulties and dangers of examinations which repress and depress good teaching are reduced to a minimum.

It will be seen, therefore, that I am hopeful that order is to come out of the present chaos, that the real facts of the existing complicated situation will be recognized, and that an educational reconstruction can be effected that will save the college for a new period of service to the highest ideals of the American people.

VIII

THE ACADEMIC CAREER

From the Annual Report as president of Columbia University,
June 30, 1910

THE ACADEMIC CAREER

The large increase in compensation to the teaching staff which has been made during the last few years has done inestimable good. The money spent upon these advances in compensation, representing as it does the annual income at 4 per cent on about three million dollars, is one more evidence of the generous and thoughtful care which the trustees have exhibited from the earliest days of King's College for the comfort and satisfaction of the teaching staff. It is doubtful whether ever before any similar action of equal magnitude has been taken by those charged with the government of a university. Indeed, while much remains to be done to adjust salaries to the new standards and cost of living, it may fairly be said that the happenings of the past decade have made the lot of a member of the permanent teaching staff of Columbia University one that is indeed fortunate. In addition to the enjoyment of the privilege of devoting several months each year to rest, recreation, or private study and writing, he has been relieved of much drudgery and routine work that were formerly laid upon him; he has in very many cases been advanced in compensation from 20 to 50 per cent; he has been given the privilege of leave of absence during half of every seventh year without sacrifice of pay, if he prefers this plan to taking a full year's leave of absence on half-pay; he has been provided with a retiring allowance in case of old age or disability, and, under certain circumstances, his widow, should he die leaving one, is also taken care of. It may be that there is some other career that is equally fortunate, but if so the fact does not appear to obtrude itself upon the public attention.

When colleges were small and universities non-existent it was possible—but very unusual—to have a faculty composed throughout of men of exceptional ability and distinction. The rapid growth and multi-plication of colleges and universities, however, has necessarily drawn into their service men of every type and kind, and of these mediocrity has claimed its full share. One main difficulty with which the higher in-stitutions of learning throughout the world have to struggle to-day is militant mediocrity. Distinction is to be sought for at whatever cost and strong, guiding personalities cannot be too numerous. But at Berlin, at Paris, and at Oxford, no less than at Columbia, the searching question is being asked, where are to be found fit successors to the scholars of the generation that is now passing off the stage? Many are sought, but few are found.

There is room in a great university for scholars of every conceivable type. The recluse and the dreamer has his place as well as the practical man who unites a love of scholarship with skill in affairs and who brings the two into constant relation to each other. A poem, a musical composition, or a new synthesis in the higher reaches of pure mathematics brings lustre to a university, as does a new invention in the field of engineering, a new discovery in the laboratory, or a new application of old principles to present economic and political needs. Freedom of the spirit is the essence of a university's life. Whatever else is done or left undone, that freedom must be made secure.

But freedom imposes responsibility, and there are distinct limitations, which ought to be self-imposed, upon that academic freedom which was won at so great a cost, and which has produced such noble results. These are the limitations imposed by common morality, common sense, common loyalty, and a decent respect for the opinions of mankind. A teacher or investigator who offends against common morality has destroyed his academic usefulness, whatever may be his intellectual attainments. A teacher who offends against the plain dictates of common sense is in like situation. A teacher who cannot give to the institution which maintains him common loyalty and that kind of service which loyalty implies ought not to be retained through fear of clamor or of criticism. Then, too, a university teacher owes a decent respect to the opinions of mankind. Men who feel that their personal convictions require them to treat the mature opinion of the civilized world without respect or with contempt may well be given an opportunity to do so from private station and without the added influence and prestige of a university's name.

To state these fundamental principles is, however, more easy than to apply them, for the answers that are made when these principles are urged are so specious and the appeals to prejudice that follow are all so plausible that their application requires courage no less than wisdom. No university can maintain its position if its official action appears to be guided by prejudice and narrowness of vision. Nevertheless, the historical development of the human race can hardly be wholly without significance, and there must be some reasonable presumption that what has been and is need not always take a subordinate and inferior place to that which is proposed for the immediate future but is yet untested and untried. It ought not to escape notice, however, that most of the increasingly numerous abuses of academic freedom are due simply to bad manners and to lack of ordinary tact and judgment.

It is the responsibility of the trustees to give to academic freedom that constant and complete protection which it must have if the true university spirit is to be fostered and preserved, and at the same time to maintain the integrity of the charge committed to their care. This must be done without either fear or favor, whatever the consequences may be.

IX

DIFFERENT TYPES OF ACADEMIC TEACHER

From the Annual Report as president of Columbia University,
June 30, 1919

DIFFERENT TYPES OF ACADEMIC TEACHER

It is quite usual to hear criticism levelled against an academic teacher for not combining in himself the two very distinct characteristics of teaching skill and scholarly initiative in research. This criticism is unfair and ought not to go longer unanswered. Of great teachers there are not very many in a generation, and nothing is more certain than that such are born and not made. Of good teachers there are, on the other hand, a fair supply. These are the men and women who, by reason of sound if sometimes partial knowledge, orderly-mindedness, skill in simple and clear presentation, and a gift of sympathy, are able to stimulate youth to study and to think. To find fault with such man or woman because he or she is not able to make important contributions to knowledge is wholly beside the mark. Very few persons are able to make important contributions to knowledge, and such persons are only in the rarest instances good teachers. It is very often true that the most distinguished scholars and men of science in a university are among its poorest teachers. The reason is simple. Their intellectual interests lie elsewhere and they have neither the mental energy nor the fund of human sympathy to give to struggling and often ill-prepared youth who may come to them for instruction and advice. Once in a long while there appears a Huxley, or a Du Bois-Reymond, or a William G. Sumner, but the number of such is sadly few. It may be said of many great scholars as Mrs. Humphry Ward recently wrote of Bishop Stubbs, probably the greatest name among the English historians during the latter half of the nineteenth century: "He had no gifts—it was his chief weakness as a teacher—for creating a young school around him, setting one young man to work on this job, and another on that, as has been done with great success in many instances abroad. He was too reserved, too critical, perhaps too sensitive." A man such as this may, nevertheless, have great influence in the background of a university and add enormously to its repute, despite the fact that his work is almost as individual as if it were done in his own study in a remote village apart from university companionship and university association. The modern university will be glad, and will aim, to find place for scholars and men of science of each of these types and of every type. There is plenty of opportunity for the skilful teacher who is not especially original or vigorous in research, and there is always opportunity for the alert-minded man of high imagination and great power of concentration who can and does make a real addition to the world's knowledge. On the other hand, quite too much attention is paid to those who when they make some slight addition to their own stock of information fancy that the world's store of knowledge is thereby increased by a new discovery.

It is quite fashionable to attack university teachers as unduly radical and revolutionary. The truth is that the radicals and revolutionaries among them are so few that they are very conspicuous. The university teacher, on the contrary, is usually very conservative, very solid-minded, and very difficult to bring to the support of a new idea or a new project. The history of the development of any important university will amply illustrate this fact. The notion that some university professors are dangerously radical because their salaries are not large enough is more than usually uncomplimentary. Such a view pushes the economic interpretation of history pretty far. The man who will change his views on economic, historical, or political subjects because his salary is doubled is made of pretty poor stuff, and the views of such a man need not trouble any one very seriously.

The most significant thing that has happened to the university teacher during the past decade is the number and variety of contacts that he has established with the practical affairs of life. These contacts were once confined to the teacher of law, of medicine, or of engineering. They are now shared by pretty much all types of university teacher. When a specialist in the Zend Avesta and in the philosophy of the Parsees is sent half-way round the world to plan relief for the suffering population of Persia, when a professor of psychology is intrusted with the task of framing a plan for the selection of officers for the United States army, when a professor of electromechanics is set to hunting the submarine in association with the officers of the United States navy, when a professor of physiography is first sent for to aid the general staff in formulating a plan of military operations on the field of battle and is then set to deciding where the boundary-line between two reconstituted nations shall run, the universities are getting pretty closely in touch with the practical events of the time. Moreover, the world at large is showing a new respect for men who have spent years in scholarly discipline and association. The President of the United States was for a quarter of a century a teacher of history and political science in three colleges; the president of the council in France once taught his native language and its literature to a group of American students at Stamford, Connecticut; the Prime Minister of Italy holds the chair of economics in the University of Naples; the first president of the Czechoslovak Republic is the most eminent teacher of philosophy among his people; one university professor has just resigned as American minister to China and another is still serving as American minister to Greece; and so it goes through other European countries and in the South American republics. The fact of the matter is that the university teacher has some time since ceased to belong to a class apart, to an isolated group leading a life carefully protected and hedged about from contact with the world of affairs. The university teacher is everywhere as adviser, as guide, as administrator; and as his personal service extends over a constantly widening field, so his influence marks the increasing interpenetration of the university and practical life. Indeed, there is no better training in practical affairs than that which the business of a modern university affords.

X

METHODS OF UNIVERSITY TEACHING

From the Annual Report as president of Columbia University,
June 30, 1907

METHODS OF UNIVERSITY TEACHING

There is a marked and healthy tendency among university teachers to lay less stress than formerly upon differences of opinion as to the relative value and importance of different subjects of study, and to devote more thought to questions connected with the most effective presentation to students of the subject-matter in any given part of the field of knowledge. It is the part of wisdom not only to permit, but to encourage, wide diversity of method on the part of university teachers, in order that the personality of each teacher may express itself most directly and most effectively in its contact with students. Methods of teaching are more largely dependent upon the individual teacher than is often realized, and while certain fundamental principles governing all teaching appear to be established as the result of study and experience, yet when an attempt is made to carry uniformity into matters of detail the result is generally failure.

In those branches of natural science which afford opportunity for experiment as well as for observation, laboratory methods of teaching have gradually developed that are particularly excellent by reason of three characteristics. They bring the student in touch with concrete facts, they afford opportunity for the adaptation of the work to the needs and capacity of the individual student, and they bring student and teacher into close personal association.

These three characteristics of laboratory instruction might with some care be carried over to instruction in quite other subjects. The parrot-like repetition of passages memorized from a text has largely disappeared from college teaching and is not to be found in the universities. Unfortunately, however, the substitute which has been too often found for the old repetition from a text-book is the lecture system which has so largely characterized, and still characterizes, the work of the German university. Of lectures as a mode of imparting knowledge, Mr. Benson, in his delightful essays entitled *From a College Window*, truly says:

> They belong to the days when books were few and expensive; when few persons could acquire a library of their own; when lecturers accumulated knowledge that was not the property of the world; when notes were laboriously copied and handed on; when one of the joys of learning was the consciousness of possessing secrets not known to other men.

The value of the lecture as a method of instruction lies in the opportunity it affords for the expression of the personality of the teacher. Its limitations are due to the attempt to rely wholly upon the lecture for imparting the desired information. The lecture, if based upon a text or a syllabus in the hands of the hearers, of which text or syllabus the lecture is an exposition, or if accompanied with or followed by discussion of the material expounded, has great usefulness. Unfortunately, however, too many university teachers rely wholly upon the lecture, without any of these additional aids, and they are not always careful to see that their recommendations as to collateral reading and study are followed by the students. The result is that by the promiscuous use of the lecture system there is an enormous waste of power and a great loss of opportunity. The power of the teacher is largely wasted because under these circumstances he is able to reach and stimulate only the most intelligent and devoted students. There is a loss of opportunity because, by more personal and intimate methods of presenting the subject-matter of instruction, the teacher might easily reach all the students who elect to follow his instruction. In some cases where the group of students attending any given academic exercise is small, a number of university teachers have hit upon very personal and almost ideal methods of giving their guidance and instruction. As soon, however, as the group becomes moderately large, there is a tendency to have recourse to the lecture alone, and the evils which have already been pointed out follow promptly in its train.

Undoubtedly, the university as a whole might do much to improve the methods of teaching followed by the staff of instruction. For example, it could, if means were at hand, provide for each department which deals with a literary, a linguistic, an historical, an economic, or a philosophical subject, equipment similar to that which is provided for the study of mathematics and the experimental sciences. It could bring together in one building or in one group of rooms the books and illustrative apparatus useful for the presentation of a given subject and thereby put the teachers of these subjects in very much the same position as that occupied by the teacher who has provided for his use a well-equipped laboratory.

It may be, too, that our university legislation is open to criticism for compelling each student to divide his attention among too many subjects of study. At the time when this legislation was adopted, there was fear lest in the newly organized university, students would specialize unduly. It is at least open to debate whether as a result of this legislation they are not now compelled to scatter their intellectual energies unprofitably.

XI

COLLEGE AND UNIVERSITY TEACHING

From the Annual Report as president of Columbia University,
June 30, 1914

COLLEGE AND UNIVERSITY TEACHING

An ever-present question in an institution of the higher learning is how to interest officers of instruction in the subject of education. They are certain to be interested each in his own particular branch of study, but much too few of them are interested in education itself. The consequence is that the teaching of many very famous men is distinctly poor; sometimes it is even worse. This results in part from the breakdown of the general educational process into a variety of highly specialized activities, and in part from the carelessness of college teachers as to everything which affects a student's manners, speech, conduct, and sense of proportion, provided only he gets hold of certain facts which the teacher desires to communicate. It is also due in large part to the bad tradition which so largely prevents the inspection and supervision of the work of young teachers by their elders. At one time the professor of mathematics in Columbia College made a practice of visiting the classroom of each one of his junior officers at least once in each week. He observed the discipline, the order, and the general attitude of the class. He intervened in the instruction when he felt moved to do so. He made suggestions and, if necessary, after the exercise was over he gave private criticism to the junior instructor.

In this way the younger man was helped by the experience and skill of his elder. To-day such a practice is almost unheard of, either in Columbia College or in any other college. With the exception of one or two departments in which better practices prevail, it is usual for even the youngest of instructors to be shut up in the classroom with a company of students and left to his own devices. The damage he may do in learning what teaching is all about is not infrequently irreparable, but no older or more experienced head is at hand to counsel and to direct him. In this way many men grow up to be poor teachers without knowing it. They are conscious of growing in scholarly power and in acquired knowledge and they readily confuse these facts with increase in teaching skill.

The late Colonel Francis W. Parker once dedicated a text-book "to all teachers who thoughtfully and thoroughly prepare every lesson." Herein lies the secret of really good teaching. The preparation of every lesson, however familiar its subject-matter, is the sure protection against mechanical routine and dry-as-dust lecturing. This applies equally to instruction by lecture, by laboratory work, or by classroom teaching and discussion. The first act of a really good college teacher is to explain to his class what it is proposed to accomplish by the particular course of instruction for which they are assembled, what methods are to be followed and why, and also why a particular subject-matter has been chosen. These opening explanations are as necessary to the intelligent student as is a chart to a sailor. The college student cannot be expected to guess correctly at the aim or purpose of a particular course of instruction or to find at once a satisfactory explanation of the subject-matter that is presented to him for mastery. To throw a child into deep water as a first lesson in swimming is not intelligent and usually leads to disaster. The student should always be told, before setting out on one of these intellectual voyages of discovery, what haven is his goal and what route is to be taken to reach it. After this has been done, the good college teacher will have something to say of the literature of the subject, of those books that will be found most helpful and illuminating, and of how they are to be judged and estimated relatively to one another. He will then address himself to the task, not of lecturing or of quizzing, but of actual teaching. A college class that is being well taught as a group is alert and attentive and every member of the group is in full co-operation with the other members and with the teacher. Facts are being transformed into factors of knowledge, interpretations are being developed and made clear, and criticisms are being fairly and frankly dealt with, there being complete co-operation and participation between teacher and taught. It is not good college teaching when the instructor merely lectures to his class, much less so when he drones to them. It is not good class teaching when the instructor deals with one student at a time, leaving the rest of the group listless and inattentive and awaiting what is oddly called their "turn." In the laboratories, the best teaching is now wholly individual. There is to be found what is known as constant elbow-touch between the instructor and each one of his students. Every student has his own particular task and he works diligently upon it, under certain fixed restrictions as to time and material, with a competent instructor at his elbow for guidance, for criticism, and for suggestion. As the student grows in maturity and power of self-direction, teaching naturally tends to become more and more individual until, in the advanced work of the university, the very best instruction in any subject closely resembles the elbow-touch teaching of the laboratory.

The two mistakes into which college teachers are most likely to fall are, first, that of failing to give the students such preliminary and introductory explanations as will serve as an adequate chart for the voyage to be undertaken; and, second, that of confusing the logical with the psychological order in the presentation of facts. The really good teacher knows that the logical order is the result of mature reflection and close analysis of a large body of related phenomena, and he knows too that this comes late in the history of intellectual development. He knows also that the psychological order—the true order for the teacher to follow—is the one which is fixed by the intrinsic interest and practical significance of the phenomena in question. The good teacher will not try to force the logical order of facts or phenomena upon the immature student. He will present these facts or phenomena to him in their psychological order and so give him the material with which to understand, when his knowledge is sufficiently complete, the logical order and all that it means. The notion that one who is a master of a subject is thereby of necessity a good teacher of that subject is only less misleading and mischievous than the notion that a subject may be adequately and properly taught by one who has elaborate knowledge of the technic and machinery of teaching but whose hold on the subject-matter to be taught is very shaky indeed.

A matter that is closely related to poor teaching is found in the growing tendency of college and university departments to vocationalize all their instruction. A given department will plan all its courses of instruction solely from the point of view of the student who is going to specialize in that field. It is increasingly difficult to secure good courses of instruction for those who have the very proper desire to gain some real knowledge of a given topic without intending to become specialists in it. A university department is not well organized and is not doing its duty until it establishes and maintains at least one strong substantial university course designed primarily for students of maturity and power, which course will be an end in itself and will present to those who take it a general view of the subject-matter of a designated field of knowledge, its methods, its literature, and its results. It should be possible for an advanced student specializing in some other field to gain a general knowledge of physical problems and processes without becoming a physicist; or a general knowledge of chemical problems and processes without becoming a chemist; or a general knowledge of zoological problems and processes without becoming a zoologist; or a general knowledge of mathematical problems and processes without becoming a mathematician. The reply that knowledge has become so highly specialized that no one can be found to give such courses of instruction is the saddest confession of incompetence and educational failure that can possibly be made. It ought not to be made except under cover of darkness.

It is worthy of note that while difficulties are found in providing general courses of instruction of the kind described to deal with a given and limited field of knowledge, there is apparently no particular difficulty in finding courses that in limpid and desultory fashion deal with everything in the heavens above, in the earth beneath, and in the waters under the earth. Last year a graduate student who was about to leave an American university made the statement that he had attended four courses of instruction given by four different persons under the auspices of four distinct departments, and that he had heard substantially the same thing in all four. This is surely a type of academic freedom upon which some limitation, economic, temporal, ethical, or intellectual, might well be placed.

Columbia University has at its doors one of the greatest and most inviting laboratories in the world. New York City is a laboratory of almost unexampled magnitude and many-sidedness. Here are courts of every sort and kind for the observation and study of the student of law; here are hospitals and clinics without number for the observation and study of the student of medicine; here are engineering undertakings that cannot be matched, perhaps, anywhere in the world for the observation and study of the student of applied science; here are buildings of amazing variety of type for the observation and study of the student of architecture; here are colleges and schools reaching directly hundreds of thousands of human beings for the observation and study of students of education; here are museums of art and of natural history as well as a zoological park and botanical garden of unusual excellence for the observation and study of students of these subjects; here is a complex and highly organized municipal government, a congeries of nationalities, a constant stream of inflowing immigration, for the observation and study of him who would know the social and political problems of to-day at first-hand. An increasing proportion of the advanced and professional work of the university should be done in this laboratory. There should be co-operation at every possible point between the university teachers and the directors of this laboratory in its various departments and subdivisions, both official and unofficial. Here, as nowhere else in America, perhaps as nowhere else in the world, the advanced student may measure the working of different and opposing theories and may see the practical results of old and new tendencies and ideals.

In this laboratory productive and inquiring scholarship can speedily test the results and proposals of these tendencies and ideals. Every year should see a larger number of graduate and professional students leaving the university filled with a new pride in the city of New York because they have come to know and to understand some one of the myriad admirable things that happen or are done there.

XII

MODERN FOREIGN LANGUAGE STUDY

From the Annual Report as president of Columbia University,
June 30, 1918

MODERN FOREIGN LANGUAGE STUDY

Restlessness under conditions that have prevailed for many years as to school and college instruction in modern foreign languages is not of recent date. The teachers of these subjects have long insisted that they were not allotted sufficient time in which to accomplish the results that they desired, while the students themselves, their parents, and the teachers of other subjects have complained loudly that no matter what the reason, the fact was that very few American college students had anything approaching an easy familiarity with spoken or written French, German, Italian, or Spanish. The new international interdependences that are a result of the war have put new emphasis upon these discontents, and it is high time that some way were discovered to meet and to allay them.

It is probable that the root of the difficulty is to be found in the conditions under which the teaching of modern foreign languages was begun in American schools and colleges. This teaching was not at first accepted as a necessary and integral part of the school and college curriculum, but was treated as an extra, and in old days often paid for as such. When undertaken in this way and in this spirit it was hardly possible for the teaching of modern foreign languages to lead, save in exceptional cases, to any very large result.

It is high time to consider whether this whole branch of instruction should not be radically reorganized and readjusted to meet conditions that are not only modern but very real.

The American college is still far from realizing the goal of modern language teaching described by Henry Wadsworth Longfellow in his inaugural address when entering upon his work as professor of modern languages in Bowdoin College, September 2, 1830. Nearly ninety years ago Mr. Longfellow was moved to say:

A knowledge of the principal languages of modern Europe forms in our day an essential part of a liberal education. . . . I cannot regard the study of a language as the pastime of a listless hour. To trace the progress of the human mind through the progressive development of language; to learn how other nations thought, and felt, and spake; to enrich the understanding by opening upon it new sources of knowledge; and by speaking many tongues to become a citizen of the world; these are objects worthy of the exertion their attainment demands at our hands.

The mere acquisition of a language is not the ultimate object: It is a means to be employed in the acquisition of something which lies beyond. I should therefore deem my duty but half performed were I to limit my exertions to the narrow bounds of grammatical rules: Nay, that I had done little for the intellectual culture of a pupil when I had merely put an instrument into his hands, without explaining to him its most important uses.

Mr. Longfellow goes on throughout this notable address to give a general outline of what he conceived to be his field of academic duty, and drew a picture as satisfying as it was inviting.

Except in rare cases it cannot be doubted that the study of modern foreign languages has been carried on quite apart from any study of the life, the institutions, the art, and the civilization of the peoples whose languages they are, save that opportunity is given to read, more or less haltingly, a few of the great literary masterpieces which a particular language enshrines. The very name of our academic departments indicates a narrowness of view and purpose which we should now quickly strive to outgrow. Instead of a Department of Romance Languages and Literatures, for example, there should be, let us say, a Department of the Latin Peoples, in which might be assembled not only those teachers who give instruction in the Romance languages and literatures, but also those who give instruction in the history, the government, the art, and the architecture of those peoples that are of direct Latin descent. In similar fashion there might be Departments of the Teutonic or Germanic Peoples, of the Slavic Peoples, and of the Oriental Peoples. The Department of Classical Philology is already appropriately named, since the broad interpretation of that term is inclusive of the history, the institutions, the art, and the life of the ancient peoples of Greece and Rome. The main thing is to cease thinking of a language as something apart or as a mere tool for technical use, and to come to regard it as a pathway leading to new and inspiring regions of understanding and of appreciation. The chief purpose in studying French should be to gain an understanding and appreciation of France, and that cannot follow upon a mere study of the language as a form and instrument of literary expression alone, vitally important though that be.

XIII

TRUE VOCATIONAL PREPARATION

From the Annual Report as president of Columbia University,
June 30, 1913

TRUE VOCATIONAL PREPARATION

The younger generation shows many signs of being too impatient to prepare for life. What is called vocational training is being steadily pushed down through the secondary into the elementary schools, and presumably it will soon reach the cradle. The old notion that a child should be so trained as to have the fullest and most complete possession of its faculties and its competences, in order to rise in efficiency, to gain larger rewards, and to render more complete service, has given way to the new notion that it is quite enough if a child is trained in some aptitude to enable it to stay where it first finds itself. Of course, under the guise of progress, this is retrogression. Carried to its logical result, it would mean a static and a stratified social order. It would put an end to individual initiative and to individual opportunity. It is not difficult to foretell what results would follow both to civilization and to social order and comfort. The basis for any true vocational preparation is training to know a few things well and thoroughly, and in gaining such knowledge to form those habits of mind and of will that fit the individual to meet new duties and unforeseen emergencies. This is the real reason why the traditional training given at the University of Oxford has produced such stupendous results for generations.

Of course the Oxford training has had, to some extent at least, selected material to work upon; but it has done its work amazingly well. Whether in statesmanship or at the bar or in the army or in diplomacy or in large administrative undertakings in business, the man trained at Oxford has won first place by reason of the character and quality of his performance. No such result has been obtained, and no such result need be expected, from a school and college training which is a quick smattering of many things. At the bottom of the educational process lies discipline, and the purpose of discipline is to develop the power of self-discipline. When discipline is withdrawn, dawdling quickly enters, and the habit of dawdling is as corrupting to the intellect as it is to the morals. The patience to be thorough, the concentration to understand, and the persistence to grasp and to apply are the three traits that most clearly mark off the truly educated and disciplined man from his uneducated and undisciplined fellow, and they are precisely the three traits which are most overlooked and neglected in the modern school and college curriculum. A school is supposed to be modern and progressive if it offers something new, regardless of the fact that this something new may be not only useless, but harmful, as an educational instrument.

With the growth of democracy the need for self-discipline becomes not less, but far greater. When great bodies of men were controlled by power from without, then they were in so far disciplined; now that in all parts of the world men are shaping their own collective action without let or hindrance, the need for self-discipline is many times greater than it ever was before. In an older civilization self-discipline was necessary for the protection of individual character; to-day it is necessary for the protection of society and all its huge interests.

Too much slovenly reading, particularly of newspapers and of magazines, but also of worthless books, stands in the way of education and enlightenment. In no field of human interest is the substitution of quantity for quality more fraught with damage and disorder than in that of reading. The builders of the Constitution of the United States and the great lawyers of the colonial and early national period knew but few books, but the books that they knew were first-rate books and they knew them well. Nothing contributed so much to the fulness of their minds, to the keenness of their intellects, or to the lasting character of the institutions that they built as their reflective grasp on a few great books and on the principles and literary standards which those books taught and exemplified. Such a task as that which Gibbon set himself over a century ago would be impossible to-day, even for a syndicate of Gibbons. There are too many books now to enable another *History of the Decline and Fall of the Roman Empire* to be composed. Productivity of the highest type is checked by the excess of facilities. This is true both of books and of physical apparatus. We could get along well with far fewer books and far less apparatus, and we should be likely to get more ideas and a higher type of human being. The universities of the world search restlessly for truth, but too often they overlook the indubitable which lies at their feet.

XIV

CRITICISM OF UNIVERSITY PROFESSORS

From the Annual Report as president of Columbia University,
June 30, 1915

CRITICISM OF UNIVERSITY PROFESSORS

A not inconsiderable part of the occupations of the president is to reply to letters addressed to him in criticism of some reported utterance by a member of the teaching staff, and in making such reply to point out what is the precise status and responsibility of an academic teacher, and what is the university's share of responsibility for his utterances. The number of such criticisms made on the part of the public has notably increased in recent years, and during the past year, probably on account of the European War, these criticisms have been even more numerous than heretofore. In most cases they are based on incorrect or garbled reports of what the person in question really said. In other cases they reflect merely narrowness of view and stupidity, or a desire to use the university as an agent for some particular propaganda which the critics hold dear. One thing these criticisms have in common: they almost invariably conclude by demanding the instant removal of the offending professor from the rolls of the university.

During the past year one amiable correspondent has attacked a university officer under the caption of a "Snake at large." The fact that the gentleman in question was not a snake but a professor and that he was not at large but in retirement, had no weight in the eyes of the writer of the letter. It appears that in this case the offense was the expression in public of a favorable opinion as to the nutritive qualities of beer. The effect of this reported utterance on the mind of the objector was to deprive him of any modicum of reason that he may have hitherto possessed. He was and still is very much offended that the officer in question was not subjected to some public humiliation and rebuke.

In another case a clergyman wrote to object to the reported utterances in the classroom—incorrectly reported, it turned out—of a professor who was described as endeavoring to destroy whatever of faith in Christianity there was in the members of one of his classes. This particular complaint did not ask for the dismissal of the professor in question, but his letter left no doubt that such action would be entirely acceptable to him.

A third and more exigent correspondent wished a professor dismissed—and dismissed by cable, inasmuch as he happened to be in Europe at the time of his offense—for having written a letter to the public press in which he expressed a personal view as to the merits of the European War that was not in accordance with prevailing American opinion. This correspondent based his demand for the professor's discharge upon the fact that he was traitorous and densely ignorant. Of course these two defects would doubtless have weight with the offender's colleagues and with the trustees if the matter ever came before them in formal fashion.

Still another complainant was an official representative of a belligerent power, who wrote to denounce a university professor as a slanderer because of some difference of opinion as to the qualifications and character of an individual whose name was given. In this case the complainant did not ask for the dismissal of the offending professor but only that he should "be kindly called to account."

All this would be amusing were it not sad. It illustrates once more how much the public at large has still to learn as to the significance and purpose of universities. The notion which is sedulously cultivated in some quarters that there are powerful interests, financial, economic, and social, which wish to curb the proper freedom of speech of university professors in America, probably has little or no justification anywhere. So far as Columbia University is concerned it has no justification whatever. That there are large elements in the population which do desire to curb the proper freedom of speech of university professors is, however, indisputable. Evidence for this is to be found not only in such correspondence as has just been referred to but in letters addressed to the public press, and even in editorial utterances on the part of supposedly reputable newspapers. The fact is that people generally have a great deal to learn as to the meaning and functions of a university. The last thing that many persons want is freedom either of speech or of anything else unless its exercise happens to accord with their own somewhat violent and passionate predilections. It must be said, on the other hand, that professors of established reputation, sound judgment, and good sense rarely if ever find themselves under serious criticism from any source. Such men and women may hold what opinions they please, since they are in the habit of expressing them with discretion, moderation, good taste, and good sense. It is the violation of one or another of these canons which produces the occasional disturbance that is so widely advertised as an assertion of or attack upon academic freedom. Genuine cases of the invasion of academic freedom are so rare as to be almost non-existent. It may be doubted whether more than two such cases have occurred in the United States in the past forty years. It is a misnomer to apply the high and splendid term "academic freedom" to exhibitions of bad taste and bad manners. A university owes it to itself to defend members of its teaching staff from unjust and improper attacks made upon them, when in sincerely seeking truth they arrive at results which are either novel in themselves or in opposition to some prevailing opinion. Here again the question is much more largely one of manner than of matter. The serious, scholarly, and responsible investigator is not a demagogue, and demagogues should not be permitted to take his name in vain.

A well-organized group of American youth such as is to be found at any college or university of considerable size offers almost irresistible temptation to the propagandist. It seems to the ardent supporter of some new movement the most natural thing in the world that he should be permitted, in season and out of season, to harangue college and university students on the subject around which he feels that the whole world revolves. Any attempt to protect the students or the reputation of a given college or university for sobriety and sanity of judgment is forthwith attacked as a movement toward the suppression of free speech. A portion of the newspaper press and not a few of their more constant correspondents are aroused to action, and pretty soon there is a full-fledged agitation in progress, directed against those responsible for the administration and good order of the college or university in question. In particular, the agitation in favor of woman suffrage, and those in favor of what is called prohibition or of what is called socialism, are most active and determined in seeking to use colleges and universities as agencies and instruments of propaganda.

It may properly be pointed out that in each of these cases, and in others that are similar, there is not and cannot be involved any question of free speech in the proper sense of that term. There is no good reason why the youth who are committed to the care of a college or university should be turned over by that college or university to any agitators or propagandists who may present themselves. On the other hand, there is every reason why the college or university should protect its students from outside influences of this sort. The sound and proper policy appears to be for a college or university to see to it that its students receive information and instruction on all of these subjects, and on similar matters that interest large groups of people, from its own responsible officers of instruction or from scholarly experts selected by them because of their competence and good sense. For many years it has been the rule at Columbia University, established in 1891, that any bona-fide organization of students interested in a political or social movement and wishing to organize a club or association in support thereof might hold one meeting for organization in the university buildings, but that, so far as clubs and associations interested in political or highly contentious subjects were concerned, all subsequent meetings must be held outside of the university precincts. This plan has worked well for nearly twenty-five years. The university has been most hospitable to clubs and organizations of every sort, provided they were organized in good faith by duly registered students. Under the operation of this rule, no serious abuses have arisen and no charge has been made, or could justly be made, that freedom of speech was in any way interfered with or limited. On the other hand, the university and its students have been protected from constant and persistent agitation, during political campaigns in particular, in regard to matters that lie quite outside the main business and purpose of the university.

XV

GOVERNMENT AND ADMINISTRATION

From the Annual Report as president of Columbia University,
June 30, 1917

GOVERNMENT AND ADMINISTRATION

Some years ago the London *Spectator* invited Lord Salisbury, then prime minister, to read to his colleagues in the cabinet the eighteenth chapter of Exodus, beginning at the thirteenth verse. The writer pointed out that in that chapter the true principle of civil administration is laid down with a clearness and precision which no subsequent writers on public affairs have ever bettered. The passage in question relates the visit of Jethro to his son-in-law, Moses, in the course of which Jethro observed that the whole of Moses' energy was occupied with the details of administration. He therefore felt compelled to protest and to ask Moses why he was so continually immersed in the details of his work. The answer of Moses was not satisfying, and Jethro at once pointed out where the weak spot lay. He said to Moses: "The thing that thou doest is not good. Thou wilt surely wear away, both thou, and this people that is with thee: for the thing is too heavy for thee; thou art not able to perform it thyself alone." This wise man went on to urge that Moses should content himself with laying down general principles of action, and that details should be left to subordinates. His exact words have not lost their consequence: "Thou [Moses] shalt teach them the statutes and the laws, and shalt show them the way wherein they must walk, and the work that they must do. . . . And it shall be that every great matter they shall bring unto thee, but every small matter they shall judge themselves; so shall it be easier for thyself, and they shall bear the burden with thee."

More tractable than most sons-in-law, Moses accepted the good advice of Jethro, and the record tells that in future Moses refrained from interference with matters of detail and occupied himself solely with those of importance.

The distinction between government and administration and the principles of good administration could not be better stated than by Jethro.   Government is the establishment of principles, laws, policies, and administration is the carrying out and executing of those principles, laws, policies.   In Columbia University this distinction has been accepted and acted upon with increasing completeness for thirty years.   The records of the university make plain that before 1887 or thereabout, the trustees concerned themselves not only with the government of the university but directly with its administration.   Since July 1, 1887, however, and more completely since 1892, the statutes of the university have put all initiative and virtually complete responsibility for the educational policies and work of the university in the hands of the university council and the several faculties.   These bodies are, by their nature, legislative, and the execution of the policies authorized by them is confided to the president, to deans, to directors, to secretaries, and to other appropriate officers of administration. Democracy in government is understandable and the professed aim and faith of most modern men. Democracy in administration, however, is a meaningless phrase. There can be no democracy in collecting the fares on a street-car, or in painting a house, or in writing a letter. Vague and inconsequent writers are, nevertheless, in the habit of using the nonsensical phrase "democracy in administration," apparently without appreciation of the fact that the words are literally nonsense. To distinguish between government and administration and then to establish sound principles of administration are no less important now than in the days of Jethro and Moses.

The organization of Columbia University is prescribed by the charter, but a reading of the charter provisions would give no idea of the practical working of that organization in the present year of grace. The charter gives the trustees full legal power and authority to direct and prescribe the course of study and the discipline to be observed. The trustees have, however, by statutes of their own adoption, long since put the first of these powers in the hands of the university council and of the faculties, and the second in the hands of the president, the deans, and the directors. There is record of but a single instance since 1892 where any exercise of the powers so committed to the council or the faculties has been amended or rejected by the trustees, to whom all such action, if important, must go for formal approval; and no case of discipline has been appealed to the trustees since many years before that date.

The present functions of the trustees, as distinct from their legal powers and authority, are to care for the property and funds of the corporation, to erect and to maintain the buildings necessary for the work of the university, and to appropriate annually the sums which in their judgment are necessary and expedient for the carrying on of the university's work. In addition, the trustees select and appoint a president and, following the quaint language of the charter, "such professor or professors, tutor or tutors to assist the president in the government and education of the students belonging to the said college, and such other officer or officers, as to the said trustees shall seem meet, all of whom shall hold their offices during the pleasure of the trustees."

In practice it is only the first of these functions, that of caring for the property and funds of the corporation, which the trustees perform without consultation with other members of the university. In the planning and erection of new buildings those individuals or groups of individuals who are to occupy and use any given building are always consulted as to its plan and arrangement. For at least twenty-five years no appointment to the teaching staff has been made, with two exceptions, save upon the recommendation and advice of those members or representatives of the teaching staff most immediately interested. The two exceptions were

cases in which donors of new endowments asked for
specified appointments to the positions which the endowments made possible, submitting in each case ample testimony to the competence of the persons named.
To all teaching positions below the grade of assistant
professor, hundreds in number each year, the power of
appointment is vested in the several faculties. These
appointments are confirmed as a matter of form by
the trustees, but there is no record of any such appointment having failed of confirmation. It seems
plain, therefore, that for a quarter of a century the
practice at Columbia University has been in accord
with those ideals of university government that put
the largest possible measure of responsibility and
power in the hands of the university teachers, and that
it is probably far in advance of the policy pursued at
most other universities of rank either in Europe or in
the United States.

As the work of university administration becomes
precise and better organized, it is better done. Funds
are by no means adequate to permit the institution of
a thoroughly competent and perfectly organized administrative staff in Columbia University, but so far
as means will permit the sound principles of administration that have been described are uniformly followed. After a policy has once been formulated and
adopted by the appropriate legislative university authority, it is intrusted for execution to an individual.
That individual is chosen for his known competence in
the transaction of business and in dealing with men.

Upon him rests the responsibility, easily fixed when need be, for the prompt and effective carrying out of the measures put in his hands.

By the provisions of the charter, all officers of administration and instruction are appointed to hold their offices during the pleasure of the trustees. Useful reflection is invited by the question why it should usually be considered so normal and so natural for a teacher to exercise his pleasure to exchange one academic post for another, while so abnormal and so unnatural for the governors of an institution of learning to exercise their pleasure to substitute a more satisfactory individual teacher for a poorer or less satisfactory one. It would seem that the phrase "during the pleasure of the trustees" opened the way to a termination of academic relationship without any necessary reflection whatever upon the character of the individual teacher. Indeed, this is precisely the judicial construction that has been given to these words. In the case of People ex rel Kelsey *v.* New York Medical School, decided in 1898, the Appellate Division of the Supreme Court, in a unanimous opinion written by Mr. Justice Barrett, used this language in distinguishing between removal after charges and removal at the pleasure of the trustees (Appellate Division Reports, New York, 29:247-8):

The decision of a Board upon charges, after a hearing, cannot in any proper sense be deemed a manifestation of its pleasure. The power in the one case is absolute, in the other judicial.

It seems quite reasonable, too, that these alternative powers should thus have been conferred. It seems equally reasonable that a majority vote should have been deemed sufficient for removal at pleasure, while a three-fourths vote should have been required for a removal upon charges. When a professor is removed at pleasure, no stigma attaches to the act of removal. His services are no longer required and he is told so. That is what in substance such a removal amounts to. When he is removed upon charges, however, he is sent out into the professional world with a stain upon his record. The distinction here is obvious and the intention to discriminate, just. If a professor misconducts himself, he may be disciplined. The College in that case deems it improper to give him an honorable discharge or to permit him to depart with the impunity attached to a mere causeless dismissal. If, however, its relations with him are severed merely because he is not liked or because some one else is preferred, dismissal at pleasure is provided for. In the latter case, it is reasonable that the majority in the usual way, should govern an act. If the former, it is just that the stigma should not be fastened upon the professor without a hearing and a substantial preponderance in the vote. . . .

Upon the other hand, the College should not be tied to a particular person who, however able and worthy, happens to be afflicted with temperamental qualities which render association with him disagreeable. There can be no good reason why such a person should be permanently inflicted upon his associates, so long as he does nothing which renders him amenable to charges. . . . The appointment of a professor is not an appointment to office in the corporation any more than is the appointment of an instructor. It is an appointment which implies contractual relations in some form of which the by-law is the foundation. The professor may leave at his pleasure; the Board may terminate his professorship at its pleasure. If the relator's view be correct, the "pleasure" is his and his alone. It would follow that he has an appointment which constitutes a unilateral contract of retention at his own pleasure for life or during good behavior; in other words, a contract which he alone can specifically enforce and which is entirely dependent upon his individual will. We think this theory is entirely unfounded.

The sound common sense of this judgment cannot be gainsaid. It would be little short of a calamity were it not possible for an academic teacher to change his place of occupation without thereby reflecting upon the intelligence or the integrity of those with whom he had been associated, and similarly if it became impossible for the governing board of a school system or of a school or college to substitute one teacher for another without bringing charges against the person displaced. Any contrary theory assumes a pre-established harmony of which not even Leibnitz dreamed and a pre-established competence which would render it impossible for any one to be appointed to a teaching position who was not *ipso facto* entitled to steady promotion and increase in compensation and to a lifelong tenure. If advancement and success in the teaching profession are to depend upon merit and not merely upon status, there must be clear thinking and definite action in respect to these matters. Security of tenure is desirable, but competence and loyalty are more desirable still, and a secure tenure purchased at the price of incompetence and disloyalty must sound a death-knell to every educational system or institution where it prevails. These are all matters of grave importance in the government of an educational system or an educational institution. They cannot be dismissed with phrases or formulas, but must be met and decided in accordance with sound principle and the public interest.

Just as seven cities contended for the birthplace of Homer, so not fewer than seven American academic wits are contending for the honor of having originated the pungent saying: "Academic freedom means freedom to say what you think without thinking what you say." There is no real reason to fear that academic freedom, whether so defined or otherwise, is or ever has been in the slightest danger in the United States. Evidence to the contrary is quite too manifold and too abundant. What is constantly in danger, however, is a just sense of academic obligation. When a teacher accepts an invitation to become a member of an academic society, he thereupon loses some of the freedom that he formerly possessed. He remains, as before, subject to the restrictions and the punishments of the law; but in addition he has voluntarily accepted the restrictions put upon him by the traditions, the organization, and the purposes of the institution with which he has become associated. Try as he may, he can no longer write or speak in his own name alone. Were he to succeed in so doing, what he might write or say would have, in nine cases out of ten, no significance and no hearing. What he writes or says gains significance and a hearing because of the prestige of the academic society to which he belongs. To that prestige, with all that that word means, the academic teacher owes a distinct, a constant, and a compelling obligation. To maintain one's connection with an academic society while at war with its purposes or disloyal to its traditions and organization is neither wise nor just. No one is compelled to remain in an academic association which he dislikes or which makes him uncomfortable. What the ancient Stoic said of life itself is true of a university: "The door is always open to any one who has an excuse for leaving."

On the other hand, academic obligation is reciprocal. The academic society of which the individual teacher is a member owes to him encouragement, compensation as generous as its resources will afford, and protection from unfair attack and criticism, as well as from all avoidable hamperings and embarrassments in the prosecution of his intellectual work. Each individual member of an academic society is in some degree a keeper of that society's conscience and reputation. As such the society as a whole must give him support, assistance, and opportunity.

The same type of mind which insists that it knows no country but humanity, and that one should aim to be a citizen of no state but only of the world, indulges itself in the fiction that one may be disloyal to the academic society which he has voluntarily joined, in order to show devotion to something that he conceives to be higher and of greater value. Both contentions affront common sense and are the result of that muddled thinking which to-day is bold enough to misuse the noble name of philosophy. One effect of much recent teaching of what once was ethics is to weaken all sense of obligation of every kind except to one's own appetites and desire for instant advantage. That economic determinism which is confuted every time a human heart beats in sympathy and which all history throws to the winds has in recent years obtained much influence among those who, for lack of a more accurate term, call themselves intellectuals. These are for the most part men who know so many things which are not so that they make ignorance appear to be not only interesting but positively important. They abound just now in the lower and more popular forms of literary production, and they are not without representation in academic societies.

The time has not yet come, however, when rational persons can contemplate with satisfaction the rule of the literary and academic Bolsheviki or permit them to seize responsibility for the intellectual life of the nation.

Neglect of one's academic obligation, or carelessness regarding it, gives rise to difficult problems. Men of mature years who have achieved reputation enough to be invited to occupy a post of responsibility in a university ought not to have to be reminded that there is such a thing as academic obligation and that they fall short in it. It is humiliating and painful to find, with increasing frequency and in different parts of the country, men in distinguished academic posts who choose to act in utter disregard of the plainest dictates of ethics and good conduct. It is fortunate indeed that, however conspicuous are instances of this disregard, they are in reality negligible in number when compared with the vast body of loyal, devoted, and scholarly American academic teachers. It is noticeable, too, that instances of this lack of a sense of obligation rarely arise, if ever, in the case of those men whose intellectual occupations bring them in contact with real things. It is only when a man is concerned chiefly with opinions and views, and those opinions and views of his own making, that he finds and yields to the temptation to make his academic association the football of his own ambitions or emotions.

It is important, too, that academic teachers shall not be so absorbed in their own individual work as not to give thought and care to the larger problems and interests of the academic society to which they belong. No part of a university system is without experience that is of value in helping to meet satisfactorily the questions that arise in other parts. The professor of law who is interested in the work of the law school alone, or the professor of engineering, of medicine, or of classical philology, who cannot find time or inducement to concern himself with questions affecting the entire university, or those parts of it that are foreign to his immediate field of interest, is doing only half his academic duty. No formula can be suggested for improving these conditions. They will be removed only by patiently pointing out, year after year, what the words obligation, loyalty, and duty mean, and by refusing to let them all be transmuted either into labels for ancient superstitions or names for various forms of personal advantage. In order to keep confidence in the ultimate achievement of a university's aim, and in order to avoid discouragement at the slow progress that is making, one may take comfort in the sagacious saying of Schiller: "Let no man measure by a scale of perfection the meagre product of reality."

One of the unsatisfactory aspects of the relations between the individual teacher and his college or university lies in the procedure, or rather lack of procedure, that is followed when a person teaching in one institution is sought by the authorities of another. It appears to give some teachers no qualms of conscience to receive and to consider an invitation from another institution without discussing this with colleagues or administrative authorities of the institution which they are serving, or even without revealing it to them. In fact, there is a certain surreptitiousness about the tendering and accepting invitations to pass from one college or university to another that is not creditable either to those who tender the invitations or to those who receive and either accept or reject them. A high standard of professional honor and professional obligation would seem to require that an institution which wishes to tender an invitation to an officer of professorial rank elsewhere, should advise the president of the sister institution of that fact; and similarly that when it is desired to tender an invitation to an officer of less than professorial rank, advice of that fact should be sent to the head of the department of the college or university in which the person in question is serving. Academic officers are very quick to resent being invited to withdraw from service, no matter how serious the reason, but many of them have no compunctions whatever in deserting their assigned work on short notice, or on no notice at all, in order either to accept service in another institution, or to enter upon a profitable business undertaking, or to give expression to their emotions. There can be no serious standards of professional conduct in the calling of academic teacher until matters like these are regarded as important and are given their place as controlling influences in shaping conduct.

XVI

MAKING LIBERAL MEN AND WOMEN

From the Annual Report as president of Columbia University,
June 30, 1920

MAKING LIBERAL MEN AND WOMEN

Few things are more noticeable in much current writing and discussion than the twisting of well-known terms from their accustomed meanings. This twisting is quite often done consciously and for purposes of propaganda. Perhaps no word in the English language has suffered more from this ill treatment than the fine word liberal. The historic and familiar significance of this term is that which is worthy of a free man, of one who is open-minded and candid, of one who is open to the reception of new ideas. In this sense the thought which lies behind the word liberal has dominated every really progressive theory of education from the time of Plato to the present day. Just now, however, the word liberal is widely used as though it were synonymous with queer, odd, unconventional, otherwise-minded, in perpetual opposition. There was a time when in the neighborhood of Boston the test of liberalism was the rejection of the Andover Creed, and possibly the rejection of the Apostles' Creed itself. Many would include among liberals those who favor all sorts of social, industrial, and governmental tyranny, which are by their very nature incompatible with liberty. An enemy of the family and an experimenter with what is called trial marriage is now called a liberal. The person who would destroy government and substitute for the political state of free men a close-working combination of industrial autocracies is called a liberal. One who sneers at the religious faith or the political convictions of others, and takes care that his attitude is publicly advertised, is called a liberal. Under such circumstances it is plainly necessary to look to one's definitions. The aim of the school, the college, and the university has often been described as that of making liberal-minded men and women; but surely this need not be interpreted to include freaks, oddities, revolutionaries, and those whose conduct carries them close to the border-line which, if crossed, would require them to be put in confinement in the interest of social welfare and social safety.

The truly liberal man or woman will be self-disciplined, and will aim to make knowledge the foundation of wisdom, to base conduct upon fixed character, and to maintain an even temper at difficult times. Considering the conditions of the time in which they lived, the ancient Stoics give us some admirable examples of what is truly meant by a liberal. We cannot afford to let this word be lost or to have it stolen before our eyes. Its application should be denied to those individuals and those traits for which it is wrongly claimed, and its true definition and use should be insisted upon everywhere and at all times. Otherwise, we shall have to find some other definition of the aim of education than that of making liberal men and women.

It would be idle to ignore the fact that there is widespread public dissatisfaction with the results of present-day education. Horace Greeley's famous classification of college graduates with horned cattle is too often quoted with approving sarcasm. The mounting cost of education, both tax-supported and other, and its diverse competing forms are increasingly attracting unfavorable public attention and increasingly arousing sharp public criticism. The qualifications of those who teach are not always spoken of with approbation. In the past it has been usual to assume that whatever is done in the name of education, like that which is done in the name of philanthropy or religion, is of necessity well and deservingly done and is to be supported without murmur. There are, however, too many signs that education does not satisfactorily educate to justify or even to insure a longer continuance of this uncritical acquiescence. What is the trouble?

Perhaps a hint of where to look for an answer may be found in the remark of an undergraduate who had been in attendance upon a lecture by one of the foremost living authorities in his field. "A very scholarly lecture," the undergraduate was heard to say as the audience passed out, but his tone was one of distinct protest that he had spent his time in listening to scholarship. Scholarship, it must be confessed, is not popular in America, and what is blithely referred to as the revolt against intellectualism is, in last analysis, nothing more or less than the revolt against the influence of those who know. It is the passionate cry of ignorance for power. A casual impression gained from the reading of some hopelessly befogged magazine or from some haphazard newspaper headline, or a response to some emotional "urge"—the newest name for appetite—is greatly preferred to real knowledge. The ruling passion just now is not to know and to understand, but to get ahead, to overturn something, to apply in ways that bring material advantage some bit of information or some acquired skill. Both school and college have in large part taken their minds off the true business of education, which is to prepare youth to live, and have fixed them upon something which is very subordinate, namely, how to prepare youth to make a living. This is all part and parcel of the prevailing tendency to measure everything in terms of self-interest. Economic explanations of the conduct of individuals, of groups, and of nations—that is, explanations based upon desire for gain or love of power—are sought rather than explanations based upon intellectual or ethical foundations. But a civilization based upon self-interest rather than upon intellectual and moral principle would swiftly lapse into the barbarism out of which it has come. An educational system based upon self-interest is not worthy the support and the sacrifice of a civilized people.

We are doubtless passing through a period of reaction in education which will spend itself as periods of reaction have so often spent themselves before. The sure mark of a real reactionary is his contempt for all that man has learned and done, and his demand that the history of human achievement be thrown away and the task begun all over again on the basis of present-day dissatisfaction and distress. The sure mark of the true progressive is his acceptance of human experience, his desire to understand and to interpret it, and his determination that it shall be made the foundation for something better, something happier, and something more just than anything which has gone before.

The underlying condition essential to human happiness is progress in the power to produce. Unless that power to produce is the outgrowth of understanding, of mastery of principles, of knowledge of past achievement, and of insight into high and lasting purpose, it will not accomplish anything desirable or permanent. For a quarter century past American educational practice has been steadily losing its hold upon guiding principle and has, therefore, increasingly come to float and drift about upon the tide of mere opinion, without standards, without purpose, and without insight. The little red schoolhouse of the generation that followed the Civil War, with its wretchedly poor equipment but with an earnest and devoted teacher who laid stress upon character-building and upon the fundamentals of intellectual training, did more for the American people than does many a costly and well-equipped educational palace such as may be seen in any part of the United States to-day. It is as discouraging as it is startling to find Henry James, so lately as 1913, describing the college town which he knew best as "utterly arid and vacuous."

This decline in educational power is primarily the result of a widely influential and wholly false philosophy of education which has operated to destroy the excellence of the American school and college, as these existed a generation ago, without putting anything in its place.   It has been dinned into our ears that all subjects are of equal educational value, and that it matters not what one studies, but only how he studies it. This doctrine has destroyed the standard of value in education, and in practical application is making us a widely instructed but an uncultivated and undisciplined people. We are now solemnly adjured that children, however young, must not be guided or disciplined by their elders, but that they must be permitted to give full and free expression to their own individuality, which can of course only mean their own utter emptiness. In education as in physics, nature abhors a vacuum. Were such a theory as that to become dominant for any length of time, the whole world would thereby be sentenced to remain forever in the incompetence and immaturity of childhood. No generation would be helped or permitted to stand on the shoulders of its predecessors, or to add something to what they had already gained. Life would then be merely an everlasting beginning, devoid of accomplishment and without other aim than the multiplication of nervous reactions to a variety of accidental and rapidly succeeding stimuli. The much despised τὸ τέλος is essential to any movement that is progress; anything else is mere intellectual, social, and political wriggling.

With the decline of genuine educational guidance and helpful discipline there has gone an increasingly vigorous warfare on excellence and distinction of every kind, which is truly pathetic in its destructiveness. Youth are told that they must exert themselves and excel, but if they chance to take this advice and succeed they are then pointed to as the evil products of a harmful and ill-organized social system. So long ago as October 31, 1888, Professor Goldwin Smith, an inveterate liberal and a keen observer of his kind, wrote to Mrs. Humphry Ward: "Over the intellectual dead-level of this democracy opinion courses like the tide running in over a flat." Under such conditions the mob spirit becomes increasingly powerful. The demagogue, the persistent and plausible self-seeker, and those who possess or can command the large sums of money needed to advertise themselves throughout the land, occupy the largest place in the public eye and actually come to think of themselves and be thought of as representative Americans. It is not surprising that at least three-fourths of the best ability and best character in the United States remains in hiding, so far as public knowledge and public service are concerned.

It is significant, too, that in this period of vigorous and able-bodied reaction the world should be without a poet, without a philosopher, and without a notable religious leader. The great voices of the spirit are all stilled just now, while the mad passion for gain and for power endeavors to gratify itself through the odd device of destroying what has already been gained or accomplished.

To get back upon the path of constructive progress will be a long and difficult task. A first step will be to bring back the elementary school to its own proper business. The elementary school being universal, well-organized, and easily accessible, has been seized upon by faddists and enthusiasts of every type as an instrumentality not for better education, but for accomplishing their own particular ends. The simple business of training young children in good habits of diet and exercise and conduct; of teaching them the elementary facts of the nature which surrounds them and of the society of which they form a part; and of giving them ability to read understandingly, to write legibly, and to perform quickly and with accuracy the fundamental operations with numbers, has been pushed into the background by all sorts of enterprises that have their origin in emotionalism, in ignorance, or in mere vanity. Through lack of knowledge of educational values, and their fear of an uninformed public opinion, the secondary schools and the colleges have very largely abdicated their place as leaders in modern life and have become the plaything of whatever temporary and passing influences may operate upon them. In the hope of becoming popular they have thrown overboard principle. Throughout elementary school, high school, and college, teachers are too often not teachers at all, but preachers or propagandists for some doctrine of their own liking. One would think that the business of teaching was sufficiently simple and sufficiently important to be kept unconfused with other forms of influence; but such has not been the case. Very many teachers are preachers or propagandists first and teachers afterward.

It is in conditions like these that one must look for an explanation of the costly ineffectiveness which is so sharply charged against present-day education in the United States. We are told that boys and girls, young men and young women, spend years apparently in study and then leave school or college without a trained intelligence, without any standards of appreciation in art or in morals, with wretched manners, with slovenly speech, and without capacity to approach a new problem dispassionately or to reason about it clearly. It is asserted that we devote untold skill and labor to the teaching of French, of Spanish, and of German, and yet the high-school or college graduate who can speak or write any one of these languages correctly and freely, or read them save with difficulty, is rare indeed; that for fifty years we have poured out money without stint for the teaching of the natural and experimental sciences, and have provided costly laboratories and collections to make that teaching practical, yet the result, so far as giving a general command of scientific method or general knowledge of scientific facts is concerned, is quite negligible; that school and college students spend years upon the study of history and yet few really know any history; that these students are uniformly taught to read and are guided toward reading that which is worth while, yet it is clear that the greater part of their reading is of that which is unworthy to be read. More criticism than was ever levelled against the study of Latin, Greek, and mathematics based upon the meagre practical results obtained can be repeated with equal force against those newer subjects of school and college study which have so largely displaced Latin, Greek, and mathematics.

In Columbia College a definite and well-considered attempt is making to overcome these unfortunate conditions of modern education, and to build a wise, judicious, and truly educational programme of study upon a sound foundation. This foundation is provided by the course entitled Introduction to Contemporary Civilization, prescribed for all members of the freshman class, and given five times weekly throughout freshman year. The purpose of this course is to give the student early in his college residence a body of objective material upon which to base his own later and more advanced studies and his own judgments concerning the world in which he lives. A result of prescribing this course for all freshmen is to make sure that every student in Columbia College has a common starting-point and a single point of vantage from which to study, to understand, and to appreciate the world of nature and of man. It is significant, too, that in this course the student is brought at once face to face with real interests and with genuine problems as they exist to-day. These interests and these problems are then placed in their historic setting, the story of their development is traced, and they are analyzed into their simplest parts. The large measure of success that has attended the introduction of this course, and the great interest taken in it by the undergraduates themselves, indicate that the faculty of Columbia College is on the right track, and that it seems likely to do its full part in rescuing American college education from the reproach that is so often heaped upon it, sometimes perhaps unjustly, but too frequently with a measure of justice that we cannot refuse to recognize.

The college faculty has gone farther and in establishing a special course of reading, to be followed through two years by candidates for general honors, has recorded its conviction that the college graduate may properly be held to some knowledge of the masterpieces in literature, in poetry, in history, in philosophy, and in science. The reading-list at present given to candidates for the degree of Bachelor of Arts with general honors includes: Homer, Herodotus, Thucydides, Æschylus, Sophocles, Euripides, Aristophanes, Plato, Aristotle, Lucretius, Horace, Plutarch, Marcus Aurelius, St. Augustine, "The Nibelungenlied," "The Song of Roland," St. Thomas Aquinas, Dante, Petrarch, Montaigne, Shakespeare, Cervantes, Francis Bacon, Milton, Molière, David Hume, Montesquieu, Voltaire, Rousseau, Adam Smith, Lessing, Kant, Schiller, Goethe, Macaulay, Victor Hugo, Hegel, Darwin, Lyell, Tolstoi, Nietzsche.

This provides a rich feast of reason, and if it is wanting in any respect it is in not sufficiently representing the fine arts, other than poetry, which have in every age been the finest flower of a people's aspiration.

XVII

THE NEW PAGANISM

From the Annual Report as president of Columbia University,
June 30, 1920

THE NEW PAGANISM

Every conceivable explanation of unrest, dissatisfaction, and disorder that prevail throughout the world has been proposed except the one which is probably the deepest and most important. For between two hundred and three hundred years the modern world has been in a state of intellectual upheaval, although there are those who think that this condition began with the World War or was caused by it. This upheaval has grown constantly more wide-spread and more severe. The forces that lie behind it have profoundly affected the religious life and the religious faith of great masses of men, have shaken their confidence in age-old principles of private morals and of public policy, and have left them blindly groping for guiding principles to take the place of those that have lost their hold. A generation ago John Fiske, in one of his luminous essays, pointed out that a necessary effect of the Copernican theory of the universe was to make the earth and its inhabitants seem so small and insignificant as to be quite unimportant in the scheme of things and to transfer the centre of gravity of man's interest to suns and worlds far more vast and far more important than ours. While the Copernican theory may logically seem to have required this result, what has happened is quite different. Man's attention and interest have been increasingly turned to himself, his immediate surroundings, and his instant occupation. Having come to feel himself quite superior to all that has gone before, and being without faith in anything that lies beyond, he has tended to become an extreme egotist. The natural result has been to measure the universe in terms of himself and his present satisfactions. His own emotions and his own appetites, being present and immediate, take precedence in the shaping of conduct and of policy over any body of principles built up by the experience of others. The wisdom, the justice, the morality of an act or policy are then tested solely by its immediate results, and these results are increasingly measured in terms of the material and emotional satisfactions of the moment.

In a world so constituted and so motived, unrest, dissatisfaction, and disorder are a necessity. Set free a million or a thousand million wills to work each for the accomplishment of its own immediate material satisfactions, and nothing but unrest, dissatisfaction, and disorder is possible.

What appears to have happened is that in setting free the individual human being from those external restraints and compulsions which constitute tyranny, he has also been set free from those internal restraints and compulsions which distinguish liberty from license. The pendulum has swung too far. The time has come, the time is indeed already past, when the pendulum should begin its swing backward toward the middle point of wisdom, of sanity, of self-control, and of steady progress.

There is no man, there is no people, without a God.
That God may be a visible idol, carved of wood or
stone, to which sacrifice is offered in the forest, in the
temple, or in the market-place; or it may be an invisible idol, fashioned in a man's own image and wor-
shipped ardently at his own personal shrine. Somewhere in the universe there is that in which each
individual has firm faith, and on which he places
steady reliance. The fool who says in his heart
"There is no God," really means there is no God but
himself. His supreme egotism, his colossal vanity,
have placed him at the centre of the universe which is
thereafter to be measured and dealt with in terms of
his personal satisfactions. So it has come to pass
that after nearly two thousand years much of the
world resembles the Athens of St. Paul's time, in that
it is wholly given to idolatry; but in the modern case
there are as many idols as idol-worshippers, and every
such idol-worshipper finds his idol in the looking-glass.
The time has come once again to repeat and to expound in thunderous tones the noble sermon of St.
Paul on Mars Hill, and to declare to these modern
idolaters "Whom, therefore, ye ignorantly worship,
Him declare I unto you."

There can be no cure for the world's ills and no
abatement of the world's discontents until faith and
the rule of everlasting principle are again restored
and made supreme in the life of men and of nations.
These millions of man-made gods, these myriads of
personal idols, must be broken up and destroyed, and

the heart and mind of man brought back to a comprehension of the real meaning of faith and its place
in life. This cannot be done by exhortation or by
preaching alone. It must be done also by teaching;
careful, systematic, rational teaching, that will show
in a simple language, which the uninstructed can
understand, what are the essentials of a permanent
and lofty morality, of a stable and just social order,
and of a secure and sublime religious faith.

Here we come upon the whole great problem of
national education, its successes and its disappoint-
ments, its achievements and its problems yet un-
solved. Education is not merely instruction—far from
it. It is the leading of the youth out into a comprehension of his environment, that, comprehending, he
may so act and so conduct himself as to leave the
world better and happier for his having lived in it.
This environment is not by any means a material
thing alone. It is material of course, but, in addition,
it is intellectual, it is spiritual. The youth who is led
to an understanding of nature and of economics and
left blind and deaf to the appeals of literature, of art,
of morals, and of religion, has been shown but a part
of that great environment which is his inheritance as
a human being. The school and the college do much,
but the school and the college cannot do all. Since
Protestantism broke up the solidarity of the ecclesiastical organization in the Western world, and since
democracy made intermingling of state and church
impossible, it has been necessary, if religion is to be

saved for men, that the family and the church do their vital co-operative part in a national organization of educational effort. The school, the family, and the church are three co-operating educational agencies, each of which has its weight of responsibility to bear. If the family be weakened in respect of its moral and spiritual basis, or if the church be neglectful of its obligation to offer systematic, continuous, and convincing religious instruction to the young who are within its sphere of influence, there can be no hope for a Christian education or for the powerful perpetuation of the Christian faith in the minds and lives of the next generation and those immediately to follow. We are trustees of a great inheritance. If we abuse or neglect that trust we are responsible before Almighty God for the infinite damage that will be done in the life of individuals and of nations.

The contacts and associations of civilized men are many and various. The two contacts and associations that have been most lasting and most influential are those which constitute the state and the church. The state is the expression of man's ability to co-operate with his fellows in establishing law, in preserving order, and, as the generations pass, in protecting the opportunity of each individual to achieve and to enjoy liberty. The church is the expression of man's desire to co-operate in worship of the object of his faith. Both state and church have a long and familiar history, and there is no need to recount any part of it here. Of the other contacts and associations of men, none is likely to be considered more important than that which has for its purpose the conservation, the advancement, and the dissemination of knowledge, together with the pursuit of truth, upon which activity all knowledge depends for its vital power. When men are sufficiently convinced that the pursuit of truth is an object worthy of their lifelong endeavor, the university as we now know it comes into existence as both the voice and the symbol of this form of human activity. When men associate together in pursuit of truth, their ruling thought is not agreement, but truth as each finds and interprets it. For this reason there will be in the university nothing which approaches agreement or unity as to matters of politics or religion beyond the fact that honest and sincere men are protected in their right to hold such political and religious views as they may choose, provided only that these are consistent with the pursuit of truth itself and with the welfare and usefulness of the particular society of scholars to which they belong. With all the good-will in the world toward an individual who might dissent from the multiplication table or insist that he had solved the problem of perpetual motion, the teachers of mathematics and of physics would not be able to find a place for him in their teaching ranks. Somewhere in the fields of religion and politics a similar line is to be drawn, but it is difficult to find, and still more difficult to apply if found.

There is no recognized doctrine of human liberty which extends to the individual the unchallenged right to take his own life. If he attempts it he is forcibly prevented, and if he attempts it and fails, he is punished. What is true of an individual is true likewise of men's associations in the state and in the church. There comes a time when dissent takes on the form of suicide or assault with intent to kill, and when, therefore, it is prevented and punished. The philosophical basis for this is clear enough. There can be no serious discussion of truth and no sincere attempt to answer the question of jesting Pilate, unless it be assumed that there is such a thing as truth to be pursued, and, if possible, found. When found and demonstrated, truth is to be recognized and acted upon. It will not do for some one else to say that he has a wholly contrary conception of truth, or that truth for him means something quite other than truth for any one else. Some forms of this genially inconsequent doctrine are just now enjoying a certain short-lived popularity based upon a false psychology and a grievous travesty on philosophy, but their irrationality and the immorality of conduct based upon them are so obvious that their life is certain to be short.

Underlying the organization of the university, then, there is a certain general, very general, agreement on a series of fundamental assumptions as to the state and the church; Columbia University, for instance, is both American and Christian. Unless a university entirely abandons its own peculiar aim and becomes merely an instrument of propaganda for some specific doctrine, it cannot in its institutional capacity properly go beyond this and be drawn into either political or religious controversy. Its individual members, be they few or many, will follow the guidance of their several heads and hearts in seeking or accepting political and religious associations and in advancing specific political or religious doctrines; but they will not, indeed they cannot, thereby commit the university to their own convictions or beliefs.

It must be borne in mind, then, that any member of a university who does his duty as he sees it in citizenship and in the religious life is doing it solely as an individual, and that his university relationship or activity is in no wise affected thereby. This is a hard lesson for some observers of contemporary life to learn. They do not seem able to understand how it is that one individual may have a variety of human associations and yet not commit them all to his own course in relation to any one of them. Clear thinking will distinguish between men's different associations, and it will be able to render unto Cæsar the things which are Cæsar's, and to render unto God the things which are God's.

XVIII

THE BUILDING OF CHARACTER

Address at opening of one hundred and fifty-second academic
year, September 27, 1905

THE BUILDING OF CHARACTER

My first word to the members of the university, young and old, must be welcome; welcome to a new year of work, of growth, and of service. Illness and death have brought us pain and grief since we parted for the summer recess, and we stand to-day in the shadow of our heavy and latest sorrow. We cherish the memory and the example of those who have gone from us, and for those who are ill we earnestly wish a speedy and complete recovery to health and strength.

Many of you are here for the first time, and we older friends and colleagues understand full well the thrill of pride and enthusiasm that accompanies the consciousness that you have voluntarily associated yourselves with one of the world's recognized centres of power. Each year will find you more appreciative of what Columbia has been and is, and of what Columbia is steadily coming to be. And as the true significance of the university grows clearer, you will gain new joy and happiness from sharing in some measure its glory and its fame.

May I detain you a moment to point out one fundamental fact? Diverse as our intellectual interests here are, and various as are our daily tasks, there is one aim which all faculties and schools, all teachers and scholars, have in common—the building of character. Whether we pursue the older liberal studies or the newer applications of knowledge or some one of the learned professions, we are all concerned, first and foremost, with the forming of those traits and habits which together constitute character. If we fail in this all our learning is an evil.

Just now the American people are receiving some painful lessons in practical ethics. They are having brought home to them, with severe emphasis, the distinction between character and reputation. A man's true character, it abundantly appears, may be quite in conflict with his reputation, which is the public estimate of him. Of late we have been watching reputations melt away like snow before the sun; and the sun in this case is publicity. Men who for years have been trusted implicitly by their fellows and so placed in positions of honor and grave responsibility are seen to be mere reckless speculators with the money of others and petty pilferers of the savings of the poor and needy. With all this shameful story spread before us it takes some courage to follow Emerson's advice not to bark against the bad, but rather to chant the beauty of the good.

Put bluntly, the situation which confronts Americans to-day is due to lack of moral principle. New statutes may be needed, but statutes will not put moral principle where it does not exist. The greed for gain and the greed for power have blinded men to the time-old distinction between right and wrong. Both among business men and at the bar are to be found advisers, counted shrewd and successful, who have substituted the penal code for the moral law as the standard of conduct. Right and wrong have given way to the subtler distinction between legal, not-illegal, and illegal; or better, perhaps, between honest, law-honest, and dishonest. This new triumph of mind over morals is bad enough in itself; but when, in addition, its exponents secure material gain and professional prosperity, it becomes a menace to our integrity as a people.

Against this casuistry of the counting-house and of the law-office, against this subterfuge and deceit, real character will stand like a rock. This university, and all universities, in season and out of season, must keep clearly in view before themselves and the public the real meaning of character, and they must never tire of preaching that character and character alone makes knowledge, skill, and wealth a help rather than a harm to those who possess them and to the community as a whole.

XIX

WORTHY COMPANIONSHIP

Address at opening of the one hundred and fifty-ninth
academic year, September 25, 1912

WORTHY COMPANIONSHIP

When we assemble the university on each recurring commencement day, it is natural for us to look back at what has been accomplished in the year that has passed. When we assemble the university on the opening day of a new academic year, it is equally natural to look forward with hope and anticipation to the new paths that are opening out before us. To such a new year, the one hundred and fifty-ninth in the history of Columbia, I offer a cordial and heartfelt welcome both to the scholars who teach and to the scholars who learn, to those who have returned to a place that is already familiar and beloved, and to those who join us for the first time. We shall at once start each upon his separate way, but we shall be animated throughout the year by a common purpose and by a common love and loyalty to the university which includes us all and which alone make possible the rich and helpful opportunities that are offered to us.

Let us each resolve during the academic year now opening to strengthen and make firmer our hold upon something that really lasts, something that is worth while, something that is raised above the temporary turmoils and vulgar self-seeking of the day. Let us close our ears, so far as possible, to the roar of malice, untruthfulness, and slander that fills the air of this year of grace.

There is one word of counsel that I offer to each member of this university, whatever his field of study and whatever his chief intellectual occupation. Resolve to pass the year in company with some one high and noble character that has left a mark on the world and set a standard which is at once an invitation and an inspiration. Doubtless many such suggest themselves; but, to be concrete and specific, I will name some that occur to me as of particular significance and interest just now.

Let the year be made noteworthy, for example, by passing it in company with the poetry of Alfred Tennyson, a poet who will one day be even more highly appreciated than at present, not only for the sweetness of his song, but for the scope and profundity of his thought. Do not read at the poetry of Tennyson, do not read about the poetry of Tennyson, but read the poetry of Tennyson itself. Commit to memory some of those passages which are at once a comfort and a delight to all intelligent persons.

Or, if in another mood, pass the year in close and familiar company with the *Essays* of Emerson. Learn from him the difference between gold and dross. Learn from him the secret of the perpetual movement of the spirit and the secret of the making of standards. Let him teach you how to think about things that matter. Go with him along the bypaths of reflection until you become familiar and in love with some of the most charming nooks and crannies into which real thought penetrates.

Or, again, if thirsting for the companionship of a life of action and of service, driven by the motive power of high purpose and a moral ideal, spend the year with that masterpiece of biography, Lord Morley's *Life of Gladstone*. In those volumes you may watch the growth of a powerful mind and a strong character through contact with great problems and large ideals. You may witness a course of education in public affairs through association with genuine problems, with real public interests, and with the highest conceptions of a nation's service.

A fourth suggestion occurs to me. The nineteenth century left no nobler or inspiring life than that of Pasteur. Perhaps you may prefer to pass the year in company with that life as told by Vallery-Radot. The history of scientific inquiry contains nothing more full of suggestion and more abundant in conquests than the story of the life of this greatest of modern Frenchmen. From that story you may learn the real meaning of the words scientific method. From that story you may learn the real meaning of the conception of science in the service of public weal.

Whether you choose as your companion of this year the poetry of Tennyson, or the *Essays* of Emerson, or the *Life of Gladstone*, or the *Life of Pasteur*, you will have an association never to be forgotten. From this companionship you will gain a centre point about which to organize your own personal academic studies.

From it you will get a keystone for the arch that you are hoping to build. From it you will get a sense of achicvement and of worth that will contribute powerfully to your intellectual and moral growth as a human being.

XX

REASONABLENESS

Address at opening of one hundred and sixty-third academic
year, September 27, 1916

REASONABLENESS

One of the chief purposes for which a university exists is thrown into strong relief by the happenings that are taking place round about us on every side. A university aims to exhibit and to teach reasonableness. It aims to exhibit and to teach orderly and judicious examination of facts and of arguments. It is averse to the use of force where reason should rule, and it deplores the overruling of reason by force. Just now force is regnant, or is aiming to ascend the throne of power, wherever one looks. In the relations between nations, in the carrying forward of our social and industrial life, and even in the dealings of one individual with another, we are being treated to unusually numerous and unusually distressing examples of the use of force. "Force," said Joubert, "rules the world until Right is ready." A true university will labor in season and out of season to make the world ready and willing for the rule of right.

A university must exhibit and teach reasonableness. Reasonableness is more than rationality; it is more than the rule of reason. Reasonableness is a quality of temper as well as of intellect. It implies the control of passion and emotion by reason, not as an occasional or unusual act, but as a general habit and type of character. The university calls to each one

of us, teachers and students alike, to cultivate reasonableness, open-mindedness, gentleness, and kindliness
of feeling, and the endeavor to escape from the mere
rule of force or from the adoration of physical and
material power. If we make this coming year a year
of growth in reasonableness we shall have done, each
one of us, what we can to fulfil one of the high aims
for which this university exists.

XXI

STEADFAST IN THE FAITH

Address delivered in St. Paul's Chapel, Columbia University,
November 28, 1917

STEADFAST IN THE FAITH

The revolving year brings us again to the eve of Thanksgiving. This glad festival, to which we are summoned by the President of the United States in compelling words, is a notable happening in our national life. For generations it has taken the place of the ancient festival of harvest-home, and has served as an invitation and as an opportunity to give thanks to Almighty God for His blessings and His benefits.

One may ask, as each year follows in the steps of those that have gone before, what is it that we shall just now be thankful for? What is it that we shall just now single out for emphasis in our own thinking and in our own worship? Is it carnage? Is it destruction? Is it infinite loss of life and toilsomely acquired property and opportunity? Is it a harvest of hate? No, it is none of these things. We could not be thankful for them, for any one of them, and hold our heads erect as sincere and God-fearing men and women.

We must, members of the university, look beneath the surface and find something there revealed to our vision which shall, like Thanksgiving day itself, not only invite but compel our thankfulness. What is it? Is it not the vision to see, the will to decide, the power to execute, and the steadfastness to continue in the faith and the power of the everlasting principles of human justice and human liberty? Suppose that there had been no people with this faith and this will and this power; suppose that the whole world, with all of its accumulations and all of its opportunities, had been left undefended, to be preyed upon by the forces of destruction, what would have been the subject of Thanksgiving day for our children? It might have been that they would have had a memory to look back upon what their fathers and their forefathers had enjoyed, but which they, alas, through the impotence of their fathers, had lost. But our thanksgiving, thank God, takes another form. We are thankful and grateful, on this November day, for the faith and the steadfastness, not alone of our nation, but of other great nations older than ours, which, more quickly than we, acted on their instincts and their impulses, and as clearly as we, perhaps more clearly, saw the great issue and proceeded to its determination.

Out of our body have gone for service and for sacrifice almost countless numbers of teachers and of taught, and those who, though no longer on our rolls, are proudly held among alumni as our elder brothers. They have gone by the hundred. They will go before the end comes by the thousand. But they will go singing and with courage in the faith and the steadfastness which are theirs and in the faith and the steadfastness which they leave behind them here.

Everything that we hold dear now depends upon the faith and the steadfastness of England, of France, of Italy, and of America. There are other allies, helpful and eager, but those peoples first in the line of civilization, of advancement, must provide the faith and the steadfastness on which the future history of free man is to be built.

May we not be thankful from the very depths of our beings when we see how splendid, how magnificent, how generous, have been the convictions, the efforts, and the sacrifices that have all indicated with convincing certainty what the issue, however distant, is to be?

But, members of the university, if we are to have faith and if we are to continue steadfast, there must be something in which we believe and for which we hold steadfastness to be a virtue. That is the answer to the false teaching that there are no principles, that everything merely happens, and that one happening is as important as another, and that life and history are like the meaningless play of the log swept in and out of the harbor, helplessly, on the moving tides of a restless ocean. Believe me, that teaching is false. Believe me, that teaching would destroy the basis of your character and mine, of this nation's life, of England's life, of France's life, of Italy's life, of the life of each one of them, for national character resembles individual character in this, that it reveals itself in conduct. It was, if I recall rightly, Mr. Emerson who used the striking saying: "What you are makes so much noise that I cannot hear what you say." Never was the distinction between conduct and mere speech more directly or more emphatically put. It makes no difference, members of the university, what we profess, unless our conduct be adjusted to that profession, reveals it, and takes command of it for fullest expression.

There are, then, these fundamental principles. I do not stop this morning to state them anew. They have been stated with superb eloquence in more languages than one and by more statesmen and philosophers and men of letters than could be gathered in this great church. We know them all, we realize them all, we have faith in them, and, for that faith, we are thankful. We shall be steadfast for them, and, for that steadfastness, we are thankful.

Just now, the effort of our enemies—our enemies of every type, the enemies of our nation and the enemies of social order and progress in every nation—is not so much now to undermine our faith as it is to undermine our steadfastness. Victory in this war must depend ultimately upon those moral qualities which persist, which shall not be discouraged by delay, by temporary check, by sacrifice, or by suffering, and which shall not be worn away by cunning and subtle pleas to our selfishness, by the seduction of phrases, or by the solicitations of demagogues. Our steadfastness, if we are to have it and to be thankful for it, must resist all those things.

Our enemies have surrendered any hope of winning this war in a military sense. The failure of their submarine attack on Great Britain, their inability to defend themselves against one thrust after another on the western front, have convinced them that, on the field of battle, this war cannot be won by them.

Therefore, during months past, they have set out to win it in other ways. They have set out to win it by cunning devices to weaken steadfastness and even to weaken faith in the armies, in the populations, and in the governments of those who are upholding the cause of human freedom and human progress. They go about with subtle pleas to selfishness, with suggestions of greater comfort, greater material gain, suggestions as to why should this loss, this sacrifice, go on, in the hope that, by breaking down the unity of purpose among the free nations, by corrupting their national character, and by seducing them from steadfastness, this war may end in a drawn battle, which is a German victory.

That, members of the university, is what is going on before your eyes and mine. It is going on in Petrograd, it is going on in Rome, it is going on in Paris, it is going on in New York. Shall our steadfastness, our steadfastness as men and women with individual responsibility and individual lives to live, be proof against this attack? Shall our national steadfastness hold out? If they do, this new form of seduction will fail as the submarine warfare has failed, and the sun of that lasting and durable peace, for which all rational men are looking and waiting and working, will begin to rise over a now clouded and darkened world.

That, members of the university, is what we must recognize. It is there that we must seek the subjects of our reflection this morning. It is there that we must look for that over which we are to rejoice and for which we are to be thankful. We are to rejoice and be thankful for faith in these principles. We are to rejoice and be thankful for steadfastness in their upholding and their execution. And then we are to see to it, each and all, that nothing happens to weaken that faith, that nothing happens to destroy or hamper that steadfastness, in order that our nation's character, and our character—your character and mine—may count in this world for construction, for upbuilding, for advance, and may not be allowed, even for an instant, by the lightest word or the most foolish act, to hamper the great and splendid progress of those ideas that are so surely marching on. And, our beloved university! When, in her long history, has she ever revealed herself more truly than at this crisis, when has she ever shown more fully and completely her great faith in these principles, and when has she ever more completely revealed her steadfastness, with an unanimity so complete as to be almost absolute? Our great company of men and women, who honor and love these two flags that hang over us, have come to give, each of his or her power or kind, to this sacrifice and to this effort. The great names of long ago! Could they come back to earth and witness what has happened here this last six months, they would clap their hands together for joy and rejoice that they had laid a foundation on which so superb a superstructure could be built.

I am to-day sending a greeting, personal in character, to every member of Columbia University who has gone into the military or naval or civil service of the United States, wherever he may be, in the hope that this greeting will reach him even when far from home and friends, on or about Christmas day. More than two thousand of these personal greetings are going out this morning. Nearly seven hundred of them are going to men and women already on the soil of France. We want each one of them to feel that, as Christmas comes and their hearts open toward thoughts of home and family and friends, Alma Mater is neither careless nor forgetful of them. Let me close what I have to say this morning by reading to you the greeting which, on behalf of you all, I am sending to each of them.

At this Christmas season when the good cheer and good-will that should mark it are so sadly absent from the lives and hearts of millions of human beings, Alma Mater has a special word of greeting and encouragement for those of her brave and stalwart sons who have given themselves to the service of the nation, even though their lives be the sacrifice. No contest in which you could possibly be engaged can equal this one in moral significance. Everything which distinguishes right from wrong in public conduct, everything which marks off principle from expediency in national life, everything which draws a line between liberty and despotism, everything which removes human opportunity from the grasping hand of cruel privilege, waits for its safety, and perhaps for its very existence, upon your success and that of the noble men of allied nations who are fighting by your side on land and sea.

Keep a stout heart, no matter how long the waiting, how severe the trials, or how near by the danger. Life will not be worth living for any of us unless you win this war. Be assured that you are to win, for the whole moral and patriotic force of America is behind you. Columbia, intensely proud of her share in this struggle and of her notable contribution of men and service to its successful conduct, sends you this word of good cheer and encouragement. When this war shall have been righteously won there will be peace on earth for all men of good-will.

XXII

THE NEW CALL TO SERVICE

A message to each Columbia man in service, December 25, 1918

THE NEW CALL TO SERVICE

To each Columbia man in service:

One year ago, when the burdens of war were new and the outlook doubtful, Alma Mater was glad to send you a Christmas message of encouragement and good cheer. To-day, as Americans all over the world respond to the President's call to give thanks for their blessings and their mercies, it is possible to send overseas a message of grateful appreciation, of exultation, and of satisfaction that the great task which was before the world in its fight against Teuton military autocracy has been successfully accomplished. Free men and free nations have shown that, given a little time, they could so organize and so arm themselves as to beat back the forces of the long-prepared and perfectly organized military autocracies. This means that freedom is safe on a foundation of strength.

We are now to prove by our bearing in the presence of the problems of the future that freedom is also safe on the foundations of reasonableness, of sympathy, and of justice. Those who have offered their lives are now to be called upon to offer their minds and their souls. The sacrifices of war are over, but the sacrifices of peace are only now to begin. These are sacrifices that will put behind us selfishness, greed, and a willingness to exploit the souls and the bodies of other men. These are sacrifices that will turn our minds

229

away from bigness, from numbers, and from accumulations, to character, to quality, and to spiritual power. We should no longer think of large nations and small nations, but only of free nations, joyfully competing together in service to mankind and in revelation of new and unsuspected powers of helpfulness and progress.

Patriotism will not be superseded by sentimentalism. Patriotism will have both a deeper and a finer meaning than it has ever had before. Love of country will not grow less, but greater, because of the demands that each country has made upon its sons, and their ready and willing response to its call. A new international order will not supersede nations; quite the contrary. It will build upon them. The part which each free nation can play in the new international order will depend primarily upon its own self-consciousness, its own self-respect, its own pride, and its own zeal for service.

You have aided, and powerfully aided, in giving to the world a peace that is to be based upon justice, and that will last so long as justice rules the hearts and guides the conduct of men. There can be no lasting peace without justice, and justice is the only sure, the safe and quick path to durable peace.

XXIII

COLUMBIA AND THE WAR

Address at the annual meeting of the Association of the Alumni at the Columbia University Club, New York, November 11, 1918

COLUMBIA AND THE WAR

Whoever selected this evening for the annual meeting of the Association of the Alumni of the College was either in the confidence of the German Emperor or in that of Marshal Foch. He either knew on what day the former gentleman would go by automobile into a neighboring country, or he knew on what day the latter gentleman would lay before the public the most minutely specific terms of unconditional surrender that the world has ever been permitted to read.

We find ourselves assembled nominally to deal with our own affairs; to discuss matters that are of immediate interest; and then we find the whole world in a heat of enthusiasm over one of the very greatest and most epoch-marking events in history. It is a little difficult, I confess, to keep anything to-night from running into the current of thought which is bearing on its bosom the hopes of the world. After all, our relation to what has been going on and to what is now going on and what we hope will go on is thoroughly typical of the historic Columbia. Despite all the admirable records that have been kept, despite the best endeavors of every recording officer to keep track of the happenings, I doubt very much whether the historian ever will be able to catch anything more than a fractional part of our university's service to the nation and to the world at this great time of crisis.

You know the lengthening line of gold stars upon our
service flag, and each one of those gold stars represents
one of the bravest and the best of the men who have
gone out from our company in the last decade or two.
Then there are stars that are happily not gold, which
indicate the service of those who are living and who
are now, fortunately, likely to escape the risk of death
or serious injury in these hostilities; but those figures,
taken by themselves, the service flag looked at by
itself, can give you no sort of appreciation of the living,
intimate contact that our men have had and are having
with every part and parcel of the conduct of this great
enterprise. What interests me most about it is that
every time a new piece of news comes, it indicates that
one of our Columbia men has had that combination of
qualities which has led him to be called upon to do
something that particularly required initiative, courage, unselfish devotion, and the power of leadership;
and those are the things which, for one hundred and
sixty odd years, we and those who have gone before
us have been striving to develop in this company of
ours, and those are the things which in very large
measure we have developed.

You cannot overestimate the service rendered by
our teaching staff. They all came promptly forward,
without criticism or demur, to meet these new and
strange and difficult conditions which have been
brought about by the emergency of the hour. But
there is even a brighter side to it than that. I have
had some of our colleagues come to me and say: "Mr.

President, I am perfectly delighted that I have been able to get into this war at last. I did not see how I could ever do it. I am too old. I did not see how I could go to Washington and take up any form of clerical work or administrative service. I am not quite suited for that, but here is a chance for me to go into the preparation of men and officers to take a part in this contest, and I am happier than I have been since the war began." That comes, gentlemen, from men who are no longer young, that comes from men whose intellectual interests and habits are remote from the kind of instruction which they are now called upon to give; but it comes also from their hearts, from their devotion, from their patriotism, and from their desire to see to it that there shall be no dissenting voice when the roll of Columbia is called by Him who takes account of national service. I can tell you anecdote after anecdote to illustrate that fact, and I ask you to believe that our teaching force to a man, from the oldest to the youngest, has asked for nothing but an opportunity to lend a hand in this enterprise.

Just now we find ourselves in the face of a most threatening situation. If I were an artist with the brush, I could ask nothing better than an opportunity to paint two pictures and to set them in contrast one with the other. I should like to paint a picture called Militarism: the Beginning, and I should like to show the German forces, armed, insolent, confident, riding into Belgium on August 4, 1914. I should like to show them trampling old men and women and children under foot. I should like to show them committing unspeakable outrages, beating down great temples and libraries and universities and churches and public buildings. I should like to show the harried city of Louvain in minutest detail. Then, over and against that, I should like to paint a picture called Militarism: the End. And I should like to show His Excellency Herr Erzberger, with his accompanying generals and admirals, blindfolded, riding in an automobile with a white flag to the headquarters of Marshal Foch. I should like everybody in this broad land and everybody in every high school and college to look on those two pictures, and then have some intelligent teacher draw the lesson and tell what it means. He could tell us of this great towering structure of Prussian militarism. He could describe to us how high it had been builded and how wide its influence reached, and how tremendous were its ambitions and its lusts. Then he could tell us how it threw itself, all panoplied and armed, against an unthinking and an unprotected world. Then he could tell us the story of those last four years and three months, ending with that picture, and show to our young men the humiliation, the shame, and the disaster to one hundred and twenty millions of German-speaking people that the architects of that great structure have brought down upon them. It has cost the lives of at least ten million human beings to bring that structure down, and every one of those ten million human beings, however humble or however great, ought to be remembered forever as a hero, because each one of that great company was part of the price that the world had to pay to get rid of this thing forever. And, gentlemen, it is gone! Believe me, there is no power on earth that can revivify it or rebuild it.

To-night we are looking out toward a new world. It is my sober opinion that the next sixty days may prove to be the most critical sixty days in modern history. We have now torn down this accursed thing, and the process of upbuilding is going to begin; and the question before every thoughtful man in this world is: Shall that upbuilding be on the lines of human experience, on the lines of human order, on the lines of human liberty, and on the lines of human justice, or shall it be an attempt to install, instead of the kaiser, the inverted autocracy of a mob? That, gentlemen, is the question which the next sixty days may decide. We saw what happened to the Slavic people when the Romanoffs fell and the bonds of a common loyalty and a common religious faith were broken and new and greedy tyrants were set loose to feed upon them. In this case we are dealing with a different people. We are dealing with the long-disciplined and the long-enslaved Teuton, and we are dealing with him at a moment of highest emotionalism. The relief which the liberal-minded Teuton might have hoped for some day in an inconceivably distant future has suddenly dropped upon him out of an open sky; and that political and social collapse which the disorderly element in society, the preying element, is always waiting for, has come without an instant's warning. The German people must work out their own salvation. Their autocratic government was unable to stand the strain of defeat, or to hold the support of people and army in the moment of disaster. The German people are, as Bismarck told them over and over again, children in politics. Whatever their accomplishments may have been in other directions, they are children in politics, and they are not ready to be called upon with startling suddenness to fill this great gap in their constituted government. Whether they can do it or not, whether they will succumb even for a time to such a series of forces of destruction as has ruled and is ruling in Russia, or whether they will rather have some such experience as that of the Paris Commune of 1871 after the disaster of Sedan, remains to be seen. But, gentlemen, the victors in this war, having been the cause of the pulling down of government, have a duty toward the building up of government. We cannot let these great peoples float about on the ocean of to-day as derelicts. We owe such assistance, such guidance, such policing, such protection as will give these wretched people a chance to get on their feet with a free government of their own. It is not to our interest to have them given over to chaos, it is not the world's interest to have them given over to chaos. That means more war, desperate war, bloody war, war not only of nations, but of classes and groups. We owe the world constructive leadership in building the governments that are to take the places of those that have been overturned. That means, gentlemen, that we should not delay one hour to make of ourselves and our Allies the beginning of a League of Nations to enforce justice and to protect international order. When those in big places say that this league cannot be formed until they meet at the peace table, they are talking what seems to me to be little short of madness. Who are coming to this peace table? Who is coming to represent Russia? Who is coming now to represent Germany? Who is coming to represent Bavaria, Baden, and the rest? There is a perfectly plain path for the victorious nations. They have been banded together in this great league. They have put their armies under one command and their navies under one command; they have pooled their financial resources, their food, their munitions, their economic resources. It is now a simple matter for them to constitute themselves into a League of Nations, not with an elaborate constitution, but with a few simply declared purposes for which they have been fighting. They can then say to the neutral nations—to Holland, to Denmark, to Sweden, to Norway, to Spain: "We shall be glad to take you into our league." Then get these new peoples who are trying to organize themselves, and whose political existence and belligerent rights have been recognized, the Czecho-Slovaks, the Jugo-Slavs, the Poles, and say to them: "Give us your programme, show us your plan; point out to us what territory seems to belong to your people because it is occupied by them or has historic and traditional rela-

tions to them.   Let us examine its economic aspects,
its elements of economic independence.   Let us see
what can be done about your government.   If you
believe in our purposes, hold your Constituent Assembly, arrive at your own form of government, adopt
your own constitution.   When those questions are
settled in the spirit of justice and sympathy and order,
we will admit you too to the League of Nations as
independent members of the brotherhood of states."
After that we can say to the Teutonic peoples: "As
an organized world, we are now ready to take up your
question with you.   You sang hymns of hate.   We
do not propose to do that.   You attacked the world.
We have thrashed you and shown you that you could
not dominate us.   Now, then, let us see what are the
elements among you for a free and orderly and liberty-
loving and responsible state; and, when you have
shown us that, whether it takes five years or fifty,
when you have washed off your hands the blood of
Belgium and Serbia and France; the blood of the
widows and orphans and hospital-ships; and the blood
of the *Lusitania* and the *Sussex* and the rest; when
you have cleansed your hands and your souls; and
when you have done those things which free and self-
respecting people must do, then we will take up your
application for membership in the League of Nations,
but not until then."

It all depends, gentlemen, upon whether we propose
to have an orderly world to go forward in progress
and peace and happiness along the lines for which this

war has been fought, or whether we propose to sentimentalize about it and to trade away the great advantages that have been won for the race and not for any special nation, and so face the prospect of our grandchildren having to do it all over again.

That is the question, gentlemen, of to-morrow. Are we ready? Have we the courage, have we the devotion, have we the leadership, to organize this world for order, for peace, and for progress, or must we, even in the slightest degree, risk a repetition of the horrors of these past years? I trust, as the world and its nations approach that problem, that everywhere, in the army of those who study, in the army of those who teach, in the army of those who lead, in the army of those who give direction, in the army of those who accomplish, everywhere there will be found the same type of Columbia man who has been carrying the flag through the dangers of war on land and sea.

XXIV

THE CONQUESTS OF WAR AND OF PEACE

Address at the Victory Celebration of the Students' Army Training Corps, South Court, Columbia University, November 12, 1918

THE CONQUESTS OF WAR AND OF PEACE

Soldiers and Sailors of the United States:

We are met to celebrate and to take note of one of the great turning-points in the progress of the human race. It may, perhaps, be doubted whether at any time more momentous and far-reaching consequences have hung upon a great decision. The decision, which was military in form, is much more than military in fact. It does not mean merely that one great group of armies has conquered another. It does not mean simply that one great group of people has subdued another. It means that one great group of ideals of human life and conduct have conquered another, a lower and much more material group, I believe, forever. The ideals that have conquered on the field of battle, that have inspired the peoples and guided the armies of the nations of free men, are the ideals which long ago took possession of Great Britain, of France, and of the United States, and to the progress and application of which we owe all that we are and all that we hope to be.

You had been chosen by the people of the United States to participate in this great contest, and you had been put in training with a view to becoming officers and leaders of men in this stupendous contest. But it so happened that, before your training was complete, before you could reach the battle-field, the great fabric that military autocracy had been so long in building has come tumbling to the ground, its foundations undermined and taken away forever. But, soldiers and sailors, just because this contest was military in form and a contest of ideas in fact, just because of that, your training has only just begun. The nation's need of your service has only been hinted at, and your opportunity to serve America, her Allies, and the free world will be far greater than we have ever known or expected.

See into what a new world you are entering as soldiers and sailors in training! You are entering into a world great portions of which must be policed, great areas of which must be held under strict military discipline and control, in order that the forces of disorder, the forces of rapine, the forces of destruction, the forces of organized selfishness and greed may not prevent these peoples from whom we have stricken the shackles of autocracy from founding their own free, liberal, and advancing governments.

We know what has happened during the past twelve months to the people and the country that once were Russians and Russia. We see signs of disorder and dismemberment in the great empires of Austria-Hungary and of Germany, and now we are to enter upon the task of reconstruction. We have had to beat down, in order that we might prepare the way to build up. Now each one of you, as an American soldier or sailor and as an American citizen, is called upon to subject himself to the stern discipline of preparation for reconstruction and for peace.

Your answer to that plea will be a test of your characters. The emotional interest, the great excitement, the tragic experiences, the tremendous risks and losses of war are now withdrawn. Therefore, without that great emotional assistance, you are left face to face with opportunity, with duty, with need for service, and your characters will be tested by your action, as your courage would have been tested had you gone overseas to take your place on the line of fire.

America has never so greatly needed as now youth of discipline, of self-respect, of clear understanding of issues and problems, of power for productive service and work. All those things are coming to you in your daily life, in your daily drill, in your daily exercise, and in your daily study. Everything that you have done will be of immediate and direct use and application in dealing with the problems of to-morrow, when you will have to steel yourselves to deal with them by force of will and without the driving power of a strong emotion which the experiences of war naturally furnish.

The world is going to have an experience that it has never had before. It is going into a year of life without a spring. The millions of youths who represented the spring are gone. Our own service flag is covered with gold stars, each one of which has wrung our hearts as we put it there. We are now about to make

a new type of service flag and to look to you men who
are going to take the places in the public life, in the
business affairs, in the many undertakings of America,
of those whom the holocaust of war destroyed, to you
and your contemporaries, the youth of your age all
over this land, to come and take the leadership in
solving the problems of to-morrow. The old men, the
tired men, may counsel, but it is too late to ask them
to take up this stupendous burden. The world of
to-morrow belongs to the young. The world of to-
morrow belongs to you. The world of to-morrow belongs to those like you in the schools and colleges all
over this land, and in France and Britain and Italy and
the rest, where they are all inspired by the ideas that
have given you your place in this university and your
place in this war.

What a prospect, gentlemen, what a prospect!
What an opportunity and what a responsibility!
Take every ounce of training that you can get. Devote yourselves day and night to the work of this
camp and this university for so many months or years
as may be needed to bring you to a point where you
are consciously ready to go out and take up your
share of the responsibility which is yours.

Then remember that you are going into a world
where men must think, where men must have sympathy, where men must have patience, where men
must know how to build. We cannot leave all that
has been destroyed to lie across the path of history as
a desert waste. We must now make it to blossom

like the rose with peoples, with industries, with happy homes, with sound ideas; and it may be, God willing, that when years have passed, it will have been your happy lot to find that you were prepared effectively to bind up the wounds of a broken world, and, under the guidance of your beloved country and your country's flag, to play a most leading part in putting this new world upon a foundation that cannot be shaken.

I congratulate you from the bottom of my heart, not only upon what this day so tremendously marks, but upon that to-morrow which beckons you to conquer it as well.

XXV

CLEAR THINKING

Address on Commencement Day, June 11, 1902

CLEAR THINKING

Over eight hundred young men and young women go out to-day from this university. Most of you will never return as students. For nearly all the period of formal preparation is now closed, and you are to prove your quality as educated men and women by the use you make of your training here. That training has been singularly diverse, and its diversity fittingly represents the broad range of the intellectual interests of to-day. Some of you have given four glad years to the liberal arts and sciences in Columbia College or in Barnard College, and are the richer in nature and in opportunity for contact with those fertile subjects of study which have nurtured generation after generation of our forefathers. Others have grown into a comprehension of the fundamental principles which underlie the several learned professions—law, medicine, teaching, engineering, architecture, and the rest—and have become skilled in following those principles to their various and several practical applications. Still others, with a scholar's career in view, led on by that scientific curiosity that is but another form of the childlike wonder which gave rise to all science, have gone far along the road toward the boundary of present knowledge in some chosen field, and have even, perhaps, experienced the thrill which accompanies the feeling that to go farther is to venture upon as yet untrodden ground. You have all, I trust, caught the earnest, helpful, democratic spirit of Columbia University, and have thereby grown in personal character and in reverence for the truth because of your life here.

Various as your studies have been and varied as your accomplishments are, there is one art in which you should all have gained practice, even though its complete mastery is still distant or, perhaps, reserved for the few. I mean the art of clear thinking.

To think clearly and straight is not easy, but by few standards can sound mental training be so well measured as by this. Clear thinking implies trained powers of observation, analysis and inference, and a balance between intellect and emotion which is not often inborn. Clear thinking can be gained only by practice. Logic is its form, scientific method is its instrument, sanity and mental poise are its presuppositions. That tranquillity of mind which Seneca has described in a noteworthy essay is an important aid. All these things your education should have brought you in some measure, whether that education has been general or special. Without these, your learning and your skill, however great, will be wasted. Clear thinking implies, too, a detachment which holds passion and temper at arm's length while opinion is forming, although warmth of feeling has its proper place in the subsequent expression of conviction. Passion for the truth is quite different from passion at the truth.

Fortunately, the pathways to the art of clear thinking are many, and each student in this university finds one opening before him. The patient dissection of a mathematical problem, of a grammatical construction, of a bit of matter living or dead; the careful analysis of a judicial opinion, the diagnosis of disease, the observation of human minds—all these lead to the exercise of the powers upon which the art of clear thinking depends. If these pathways be trodden for four years or even for a shorter time, the student has gained thereby a precious intellectual possession which outweighs any amount of variety of mere information.

The skilful authors of the *Port Royal Logic*, the precepts of which have had much to do with the exquisite order, precision, and clearness which characterize the scientific and literary expositions of the writers of modern France, pointed out no fewer than nine different ways of reasoning ill. To be avoided, these ways of reasoning ill must be known, in order that they may be recognized in one's own mental processes. For these and other practical matters which affect the art of clear thinking, and its opposite, I commend to you the admirable tract on *The Conduct of the Understanding* by the philosopher Locke. For the student who cares for clear thinking—and what student does not?—and who wishes to avoid slovenliness and inaccuracy of mind, it is perhaps the most useful book in the English language. I wish that each of you might not only read it, but own it and open it often. As a guide to the understanding of one's own mental processes and states and to a knowledge of the obstacles and aids to clear thinking, this little book of a hundred pages seems to me to have no equal. Hallam said of it years ago that it gives the reader "a sober and serious, not flippant or self-conceited, independency of thinking."

Be assured, too, that clear thinking lies at the basis of the art of expression. He who cannot explain does not wholly understand. He who fully understands has taken the first long step toward attaining the power to make known. Columbia would gladly make the art of clear thinking and the power of lucid and elegant expression the mark of her sons and daughters. That you have gained something, much, in each of these directions, we hope and we believe. Do not relax your vigilance in after years, but help these good habits to become positively irresistible through constant and adequate exercise.

You take with you, each and all, the sincerest goodwill of the university of which you have been student-members and to which you will ever belong. May you be equal in all ways to the high demands of a life which is, in the words of Burke, a life of manly, moral, regulated liberty!

XXVI

THE GOSPEL OF HOPE

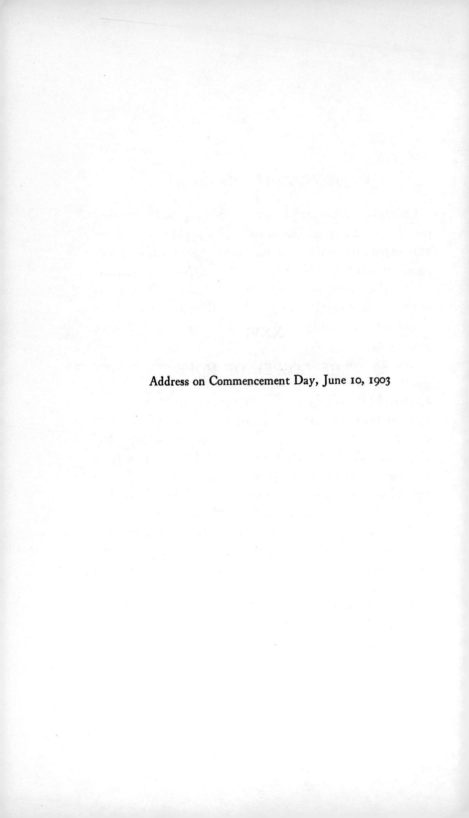

Address on Commencement Day, June 10, 1903

THE GOSPEL OF HOPE

Columbia University parts to-day with another goodly company of her sons and daughters. Regret and expectancy are, I doubt not, the feelings uppermost in your minds; hope and confidence are those which the university cherishes for you. Your presence here is a mark that you have done what has been asked of you academically, and the future lies with you alone.

Let me lay stress for a moment or two upon the point of view from which your work in life is to be approached. There is, I feel sure, neither happiness nor usefulness to be found in cultivating indifference, cynicism, or pessimism. There are those who feel that the educated youth of our land are apt to hold themselves aloof from popular interests and movements, and to view from one side, or from above, the active life of our democracy. This impression is not, I think, a just one; at all events, it is certainly less well founded now than ever before; but such foundation as it has should be rudely taken from it by your efforts and by your careers. If education and training are to unfit men, mentally, for sympathetic participation in the every-day life of the nation, then the less of education and training that we have, the better. In that case we are starving the soul to feed the mind.

But the education of to-day is not of that sort. It is insistent in its demands for practical application, for service, for human sympathy. It implies faith in God and in man, and joyous participation in human efforts.

There is no true life-gospel but the gospel of hope, the gospel of belief; not that all is as right as it can be, but that all is righteous and can be made more righteous still. Carl Hilty, in his charming essay on *Happiness*, has truly said that "Pessimism as a permanent habit of mind is, for the most part, only a mantle of philosophy through which, when it is thrown back, there looks out the face of vanity;—a vanity which is never satisfied and which withholds one forever from a contented mind." The vain, the self-centred man is at bottom a cynic, for even his own self-satisfaction is not perfect.

This university would put upon its graduates the stamp of earnestness, not paltering; of enthusiasm, not indifference; of hope and cheerfulness, not despair and gloom; of active interest in our fellow men, and not supercilious contempt for them and their affairs. Do not fear to be in earnest, and pay no heed to the whisper that it is "bad form" to be enthusiastic. Be human; be real.

Nearly forty years ago Thomas Carlyle made a famous address to the students of Edinburgh as Lord Rector of the university. It abounded in wisdom and common sense, and its advice to the Edinburgh students is comprised in the one sentence: Be diligent. But Carlyle went on to tell what he meant by diligence. It included, he said, all virtues that a student can have, all those qualities of conduct that lead on to the acquirement of real instruction and improvement. Most of all, it included honesty, intellectual as well as moral honesty. "A dishonest man cannot do anything real." That is a fine sentence and a true one; it may be paraphrased by saying that character makes knowledge worth while.

I would rather have this great company of students face the world with cheerfulness and hope and with complete honesty than endowed in any other way.

You go out to-day from under the shadow of a great tradition. For nearly a century and a half it has been slowly forming. Lives without number have been built into it. The years have crowned it with power and with beauty. It is a branch of something far older, that runs back till it loses itself in the beginnings of things. It marks the rise and dominance of the human spirit. Here you have come under its influence; here you have caught something of its meaning.

May you each in his own way be a bearer of the tradition which you have come to know. May you all find usefulness, and if it be God's will, happiness also. Mere success, as the world judges success by outward signs, I pass by. It is not worth having save as an incident to usefulness.

XXVII

PERSONAL RESPONSIBILITY

Address on Commencement Day, June 8, 1904

PERSONAL RESPONSIBILITY

It is an anxious moment when an engine, long in building, is finally to be put to its practical test. Will it work? Was its plan well made and was it wisely executed? The steam is let into the cylinder, the piston-rod moves, and the wheels begin to turn. The machine works, and the labor put upon it is worth while. The behavior of the machine in practice is the supreme test of the wisdom and skilful execution of its plan.

What is true of an engine is yet more true of men and women. The university scans closely the faces of those who pass out of its gates from year to year, in order that it may, if possible, forecast the future. Will these men and women work in practice? Has their training been wisely planned and skilfully executed? If so, the university has done its part. But one crucial question remains. Can and will each individual student who bears the university's name, worthily use the training it has given him? This is the question of personal responsibility, and it cannot be shirked.

It is not at all hard to bring home the feeling of responsibility in the abstract, but it is often a matter of extreme difficulty to enforce it in the concrete. We are always ready to legislate standards for others, but not so quick to apply them to ourselves. I hold a feeling of high responsibility to God and to man for the use of one's knowledge and training, to be an essential part of an education that is genuine. Subtract that feeling, and the most cunningly contrived intellect becomes an engine without a governor. With it, even an imperfect intellectual machine will accomplish useful results.

The college and university graduates of to-day need to reflect long and earnestly upon their responsibility. The parable of the talents applies to them. They must give some return for what has been so freely given to them. Moreover, they must feel the responsibility for giving this return, and must act upon it.

These graduates owe to themselves and to their community many things. One is intellectual honesty. You who have studied logic and you who have applied scientific method to the solution of innumerable problems know the relation between premise and conclusion, and you know that the truth-loving and truth-seeking mind will not permit contradiction between the one and the other. It is your bounden duty to exemplify this in practical life. Fashion, fear, ambition, avarice, all will tempt you to deny your honest beliefs. If you yield, your education here is in so far imperfect or you thereby renounce your responsibility for the use to which you put that education.

It might be said of responsibility, as Emerson said of truth, that you cannot have both it and repose. You must choose between them. "He in whom the love of repose predominates will accept the first creed, the first philosophy, the first political party he meets,—

most likely his father's. He gets rest, commodity and reputation; but he shuts the door of truth." So also he shuts the door of responsibility. Whatever his be-belief, in action—or rather inaction—he denies responsibility.

No educated man can afford to prefer repose to responsibility. He must act continually and courageously, and with all the light that his education has given him. Then and then only can he approach an understanding of the meaning of the high praise that Matthew Arnold gave to Sophocles:

> Who saw life steadily, and saw it whole.

There is a university visible and a university invisible. The one is made up of these stately buildings, of the throng of teachers and students, of these recurring ceremonials. The other exists in the spirit which animates the whole and which, overpassing these near bounds, inspires and guides the thousands who have gone out from us. To-day you are crossing the line beyond which lies the university invisible. Over there you are none the less in and of Columbia than you have been while here. Henceforth it is yours to share the responsibility for that school of the higher learning which was called into being a century and a half ago, not only to promote a liberal education but to make that education "as beneficial as may be."

XXVIII

THINKING FOR ONE'S SELF

Address on Commencement Day, June 14, 1905

THINKING FOR ONE'S SELF

Matthew Arnold is responsible for a significant story of the poet Shelley. Mrs. Shelley was choosing a school for her son and asked the advice of a friend. The reply was: "O! Send him somewhere where they will teach him to think for himself"; to which Mrs. Shelley answered: "Teach him to think for himself! Teach him rather to think like other people." Which is the easier, and which the more important?

The late provost of Trinity College, Dublin, Doctor George Salmon, learned alike in mathematics and theology, found no difficulty in coming to a prompt conclusion: "The labor of forming opinions for themselves," he once wrote, "is too much for most men and for almost all women. They look out for some authority from whom they can take opinions ready made, and people value their opinions by a different rule from that according to which they value their other possessions. Other things they value in proportion to the trouble it has cost them to come by them; but the less labor of their own they have bestowed in forming their opinions, the greater their scorn for those who do not covet them, the greater their indignation against those who try to deprive them of them."

These quotations put strikingly before us the time-old problem of the behavior of the individual in the presence of the mass. In one form or another this problem has perplexed the human mind for nearly three thousand years. The ancient moral philosophers, the schoolmen of the Middle Ages, the logicians, moralists, and scientists of to-day, have all struggled and are all struggling with this same problem in one or another of its aspects.

Reduced to its lowest terms and applied to the concrete interests of the moment, our question is this: Shall the university so train its students that they think for themselves or that they think like other people?

Let us choose the first alternative. The university shall so train its students that they think for themselves. Confident and jaunty the happy company of students go out into the work of the world. Each thinks for himself. Here and there is one who is sternly logical and who will not be denied the conclusions that follow from his premises. He thinks for himself in regard to some questions of public order, some questions of property, some questions of responsibility and liability. The heavy hand of the law is suddenly laid upon his shoulder and he is haled to a prison or to an asylum for lunatics. His protest that he is an educated man, thinking for himself, is unsympathetically jeered at. He is so individual that he is a nuisance and a danger, and the community suppresses him at once. Apparently, then, our choice was a wrong one, and the university should not teach men and women to think for themselves.

Let us turn to the second alternative. The university should so train its students that they think like other people. Cast in one mould, they step across Alma Mater's portals, outward bound, conventionalized, and ready to do homage to what Goethe so felicitously describes as

Was uns alle bändigt, das Gemeine.

For them whatever is, is right, and the only progress is to stand still. For some reason or other, this result fails to satisfy as an ideal, and we cannot resist the conclusion that, after all, it is not enough for the university to train its students to think like other people.

Idiosyncrasy and convention, then, are alike unsatisfactory, and we travel back to the wisdom and human insight of Aristotle for a clew to the escape from our dilemma. "Excess and deficiency," he said, "equally destroy the health and strength, while what is proportionate preserves and augments them."

The university is to train men and women—this means—in part to think for themselves and in part to think like other people. They must think like other people sufficiently to make their thinking for themselves worth while. They must have a fulcrum for their lever, and that fulcrum is the common apprehension and comprehension of the lessons of past human experience, particularly as that experience crystallizes into the institutions of civilization. The world and human society cannot now be built over just as if no plan had been prepared, no foundation laid, no work already done. It is society formed which must be taken as the basis for society reformed. It is from this year of grace and not from the creation that he who is to think for himself must take his departure. The university must in so far train its students to think like other people; this much assured, it must then train its students to think for themselves.

As persons you are raised above the domain of things and into a dominion of your own. Persons must look with their own eyes, judge with their own minds, act with their own wills. To stand up to the full measure of manhood or womanhood is task enough for any one, and it is the business of the university to train you for that task by teaching you first to think like other people and then to think for yourselves. Mrs. Shelley's mother instinct guided her aright as to where to lay the emphasis in the education of the erratic genius who was her son. For him to learn to think like other people was more important than to learn to think for himself. For most of us the reverse is true. I am confident that the university has in one form or another pressed this lesson upon you all.

For the older members of the university I extend to these younger ones hearty congratulations and every good wish for the years that are to come. May you always look back upon the years spent here as the happiest and most fruitful of your useful lives.

XXIX

THE SPIRIT OF UNREST

Address on Commencement Day, June 13, 1906

THE SPIRIT OF UNREST

For the American of ambition and education who would use his powers to best advantage in the service of his country and of humanity, there is no book of instruction equal in value to the life of Abraham Lincoln. That life tells the story of a noble soul nurtured from humblest beginnings by severe self-discipline, by contact with men, by constant occupation with large human interests and with lofty thoughts; a soul endowed with "a patience like that of nature, which in its vast and fruitful activity knows neither haste nor rest." Tested and tried as never ruler was before, distraught with conflicting counsel and urged hither and yon by every powerful influence, Lincoln's nature never lost its poise nor his judgment its clear-sighted sanity. He saved a nation because he remained tranquil amid angry seas.

This great company of graduates goes out from the university into the active work of the world at a particularly important and critical time. Unless all signs fail, we are entering upon a period of social and economic, perhaps even of political, reconstruction. A spirit of unrest is abroad, not only in our own land, but in other lands as well. So far as this unrest has an intellectual foundation, it appears to be the conviction that the eighteenth-century formulas and axioms upon which our social and political fabric is so largely built do not work as they were expected to work. So far as this unrest has an economic foundation, it appears to be dissatisfaction with actual and possible rewards for industry. So far as it has a political foundation, it appears to be a perception of easily demonstrated inequalities of power and influence and of an equally easily demonstrated inequality of benefits from governmental policies.

That this unrest has been and is being used by ambitious men for their own selfish ends and for gain by journalistic builders of emotional bonfires is certainly true; but it will not do to dismiss this spirit of unrest with a sneer on that account.

It has passed far beyond the bounds of the dreamers and visionaries, the violent-minded, and the naturally destructive. Men accustomed to honest reflection and themselves possessed of property, always the sheet-anchor of conservatism, have come under its influence. Policies that not long ago were dismissed as too extreme for serious discussion are now soberly examined with reference to their immediate practicability. What has brought about this change?

An answer is not far to seek. An increasing number of men have come to distrust the capacity of society as now organized to protect itself against the freebooters who exist in it. An increasing number of men believe and assert that law and justice are powerless before greed and cunning, and they are the more ready to listen to advocacy of any measure or policy, however novel or revolutionary, that promises relief. Their imaginations, too, cannot help being affected by the appalling sight, so often called to our attention of late, of that moral morgue wherein are exposed the shrivelled souls and ruined reputations of those who have lost in the never-ending struggle between selfishness and service that goes on in the human breast.

Where amid all this shall the university graduate throw his influence?

The first duty of the trained and educated mind when it faces conditions such as these and must take a definite and responsible attitude toward them is not to lose its balance, its poise, its self-control. It is worth while to look back at the majestic figure of Lincoln, crowned now with immortality's laurel, tranquil amid far angrier seas than ours.

Not much is to be gained by passionate denunciation of principles and men, if there is no clear perception of where the difficulty lies and of what it is that is to be remedied. A first step, then, is an analysis of the conditions complained of and their genesis. I lay particular emphasis upon their genesis, for most re-builders of society are singularly neglectful of history. Their lip-service of evolution does not often carry them to the point of considering our present institutions—social, economic, political—as evolved, and, therefore, as having the weight of years and human experience behind them.

Looking back over a thousand years or more, it is plain that civilized man has travelled far. An examination of his progress will show, I think, that it rests mainly upon three principles, gradually evolved and erected into institutions: Civil and industrial liberty, private property, and the inviolability of contract. Upon these as a corner-stone rests what we know to-day as civilized human society. That our society has its evils, terrible and dangerous, cannot be denied. That greed for gain holds an appalling number of men in its grasp and that the moral tone of large business undertakings is painfully low are only too evident. But it is quite too rash a conclusion to infer that society must be destroyed and its corner-stone displaced before those evils can be remedied. It may be true— and I think it is—that the difficulty is not so much with the tried and tested principles upon which society rests as with the honesty and intelligence with which those principles are worked. The abounding prosperity of our country with its untold opportunities for material success, the loosening of the hold of some of the old religious and ethical sanctions of conduct, and the weakening of parental control and discipline, have united to place upon American character a burden which in too many instances it has not been able to bear.

It is our own individual characters that are at fault and not the institutions whose upbuilding is the work of the ages. Sound and upright individual human characters will uplift society far more speedily and surely than any constitutional or legislative nostrum or the following of any economic or philosophical will-o'-the-wisp. Unethical acts precede illegal ones and speedily lead to them. Given an acute perception of the difference between right and wrong, a clear conception of duty, and an appreciation of the solemn obligations of a trust, our social and political system would, perhaps, be found to work equitably and well. Without these traits no system is workable. Moral regeneration, not political and economic reconstruction, is what we chiefly need.

This view of our present-day problems I press upon you with all the emphasis at my command. Most of all I ask you to keep your balance and poise in the presence of excitement and turmoil, and to learn well the lesson of him who led men—

> "By his clear-grained human worth,
> And brave old wisdom of sincerity"

—Abraham Lincoln.

XXX

LYNCH–LAW

Address on Commencement Day, June 12, 1907

LYNCH-LAW

A Virginia planter of the eighteenth century, himself a Quaker, and so, presumably, a lover of law and order and peace, has given his name to that mode of summary punishment, without due authority, which is everywhere known as lynch-law. The word to lynch may properly be extended to cover not only summary acts without warrant of law, but summary judgments without due knowledge of the facts. In this sense the lynching habit is both wide-spread and growing. Men and women of education and sound training may well be put on their guard against it.

The mad rush of our contemporary life, the haste to pass on to something new and more exciting, the daily press with its hectic head-lines and its guillotine-like opinions, all assist us to form the habit of acting and judging without thinking. It is amazing how large a part of our every-day mental attitudes, whether as to men or public policies or passing events, are the result of the lynching habit. A passage from a public address, torn loose from its setting; a partial or partisan presentation of a political act or measure; or a distorted and inaccurate account of some important happening, will serve to fix our permanent attitude toward a man or an event, and we may never know how hopelessly inadequate or erroneous the grounds for that attitude are. We pass on in blind error to still other and more confident lynchings.

The training that a university offers is the surest corrective of the lynching habit. In the laboratory, the lecture-room, and the seminar, facts are carefully collected and sifted and weighed, and final judgment is held in suspense until the process is ended. Even then the judgment is held subject to the discovery of new evidence. This mental state is not one of uncertainty, but of open-mindedness. Open-mindedness and the habit of reserving judgment until the facts are established will soon rid our natures of the lynching habit and its deplorable intellectual and moral effects. To set this example to others is just now a duty that is heavily incumbent on men and women of university training.

The lynching habit also finds support in the present-day demand for immediate and tangible results, no matter how difficult the problem or how involved the process. This demand is in itself highly irrational. In his invaluable essay *On Compromise* John Morley calls attention to the wholly unwarranted impatience at the slowness of social and political and intellectual change. "People seldom realize," he says, "the enormous period of time which each change in men's ideas requires for its full accomplishment. We speak of these changes with a peremptory kind of definiteness, as if they covered no more than the space of a few years. . . . Yet the Reformation is the name for a movement of the mind of northern Europe, which went on for three centuries. Then if we turn to that still more momentous set of events, the rise and establishment of Christianity, one might suppose that we could fix that within a space of half a century or so. Yet it was at least four hundred years before all the foundations of that great superstructure of doctrine and organization were completely laid. . . . We lose the reality of history, we fail to recognize one of the most striking aspects of human affairs, and above all we miss that most invaluable practical lesson, the lesson of patience, unless we remember that the great changes of history took up long periods of time which, when measured by the little life of a man, are almost colossal, like the vast changes of geology."

To resist the tendency to lynch-law judgments of men and things and to cultivate that admirable intellectual patience which is a sure attribute of wisdom are excellent undertakings for us all. Especially are they excellent undertakings for those who, like this great company of college and university graduates, are now to be held responsible by their Alma Mater and by the community at large for their use of the training they have received and the opportunities they have enjoyed.

XXXI

CONTACT WITH THE FIRST-RATE

Address on Commencement Day, May 27, 1908

CONTACT WITH THE FIRST-RATE

The goodly company that to-day goes out from these walls with the tokens of Alma Mater's satisfaction and approval looks almost of necessity forward. New and strange tasks are now to be begun and life's careers are now to be entered upon. Our university is to be justified, or not, of her children according as these tasks are performed and these careers accomplished. How shall each one of you know ten years hence, or twenty, whether he is still growing in nature and in spirit, and whether he is really doing things that are worth while in the world? This question implies that there are standards by the application of which we are able to determine whether the answer is to be yes or no.

There is no revelation of character, of its solidity or its hollowness, like that of the standard to which one resorts for the test of excellence. These standards are to be chosen with full recognition of the high significance of the choice, and when chosen they are to be treasured as their value deserves. Our standards of physical measurement are carefully kept from exposure to heat and cold, to dust and disturbance, that their accuracy may not be impaired. Just so are our standards of intellectual and moral measurement in need of protection. They, too, suffer from abuse, from misuse, and from exposure, and when they so suffer the results are in high degree unhappy.

A university has done but poorly for the student if it has not given him safe and enduring standards for the measurement of intellectual and moral excellence. The educated man or woman should know, and therefore should shun, the sham, the tawdry, the pretentious, and the second-rate. Nothing is so health-giving to the human spirit as constant association with what is truly first-rate. In reading the story of the life of Gladstone, one can almost see his nature grow deeper and stronger and broader through contact with noble aspiration, with large problems of public concern, with the most excellent books, and with the most elevated spirits of his time. So, in lesser degree, it may be for each one of us. If we choose the excellent and abide by it, the excellent will reward us with its gifts of power and satisfaction.

A most persistent enemy of sound standards is the tendency to delight in the applause of the crowd, and in the acclaim of the unthinking, the immature, and the ill-informed. More than one leader of men, past and present, has been led astray by the strong temptation which this tendency offers. Sometimes one almost feels that the noisiest policy is to pass for the best, and that that which is at the moment the most popular is to be adjudged the wisest. This confusion is the chief danger to which democracy is exposed. What men want often contradicts what men ought to have, and to bring the two into harmony is the supreme task alike of education and of statesmanship. Not the clamor of the crowd, however angry or however emphatic, but what Sir Thomas Browne quaintly called "the judgment of the judicious," is the true standard of merit. To it we must constantly and hopefully repair. We should never be tempted or cajoled or frightened into deserting it. Moreover, we soon learn that time is an element in all weighty judgments as to the excellence of human endeavor. If it be true that distance lends enchantment to the view, it is also true that distance gives a sense of true proportion and perspective, and an opportunity to take notice of the consequences of actions and undertakings.

Many lives that promise well end in disappointment or worse. Observation of the activities of men seems to warrant the belief that the promise of twenty or twenty-five is not often fulfilled at forty or forty-five. Each human life appears to be projected into view with a certain initial velocity and a certain potential energy, and the trajectory of most lives, even those from which much is expected, tends to bring them, through loss of initiative, to the level of assured mediocrity by forty or forty-five years of age. Length of years and capacity for achievement seem to stand in little, or at least in no direct, relation to each other. The lesson is plain. When the serious business of life is begun few men find time or inclination to refresh the spirit and to restore its energy, and so for many human beings any but the most routine existence comes to an end when the original store of potential energy is exhausted. On the other hand, the life whose potential energy is constantly renewed and increased by helpful service, by sober reflection, and by continued study, may, and will, continue to keep its trajectory high above the ground for decade after decade.

What has been done here at the university by way of preparation, and for the nurture of mind and character, is not an end, but a beginning only. To stop now storing up energy, and material convertible into energy, means that the really useful part of your lives will be over in another score of years. The present stock of intellectual fuel will then be exhausted in all but a very few cases in each thousand.

Both ambition and the instinct of self-preservation unite, therefore, in insisting that we shall labor to keep ourselves intellectually and morally alert, that we shall not exhaust our powers or let them rust through neglect, but that we shall so use them that they constantly gain in effectiveness as experience heightens their possibilities. To do this is to gain success in life, whether one's place in the world be conspicuous or humble.

Refreshment and vigor of mind and spirit will come most surely from observance of those ancient words of counsel, than which none are wiser:

Whatsoever things are true, whatsoever things are honorable, whatsoever things are just, whatsoever things are pure; whatsoever things are lovely, whatsoever things are of good report; if there be any virtue and if there be any praise, think on these things.

XXXII

INTEGRITY

Address on Commencement Day, June 2, 1909

INTEGRITY

One of the best known of the *Odes* of Horace is that which begins with the line

Integer vitæ scelerisque purus.

Whether the poet was serious, or, as some think, in a jocular vein, when he wrote this ode, makes little difference; his famous line has been read for centuries in tribute to integrity.

What higher reward can come to a man than to have it justly said of him that he possessed integrity? This means that his nature was upright, sound, complete; that there were no great gaps in his moral armor, and no weak spots in his stock of intellectual convictions. The man who possesses integrity must not only be incorruptible—that goes without saying; he must also be just, clear-sighted, and wise with the wisdom which attaches to a tried experience.

Lack of moral integrity is as sad as it is common. Sometimes it is one solicitation, sometimes another, which successfully assails a man's completeness and leaves him imperfect, broken, soiled. Lack of intellectual integrity is no less sad. It implies the absence of a body of principles on which one's knowledge and convictions rest. It implies a lack of stability of purpose; a fitfulness, which leaves one to be borne hither and yon by the blasts of temporary opinion or by the forces of everlasting selfishness.

The training which a university gives is poor stuff indeed if it has not asserted integrity alike of mind and of character as an attainable ideal, and if it has not aided in its upbuilding.

There is a subtle and often clever type of mind whose activity does great damage to integrity by its narrow distinctions, its cunning splitting of hairs, and its constant asserting of half-truths in place of that whole truth and nothing but the truth which integrity loves. One may learn the lesson of integrity if he will but open his eyes and look nature in the face; or read history with insight and appreciation; or move among men as they go about the work of the world, and watch the building up and the falling down of human character.

There is no substitute to be found for integrity; money will not buy it, nor will any accumulation, however vast, remove the stain of its opposite. It is one of man's most precious possessions and it will be sought by high-minded and confident youth with all the earnestness and vigor of their being.

Integrity has its standards, and precious, time-old standards they are. It will not be deceived by fraud and hypocrisy appearing before it in the garb of honesty and frankness; nor will it be misled by selfishness, calling in imitation of the stern voice of duty.

The world is full of men who possess moral integrity in abundance, but who are sadly lacking in integrity

of the intellect. They have never learned the real
meaning of the words principle and conviction. They
do not know that the man of integrity cannot at one
and the same time cherish contradictory opinions or
pursue mutually exclusive aims. Their natures lack
wholeness. They are composite men, made, like
Joseph's coat, of many colors. The solid, substantial
unity of mind which comes from applying to each
problem as it arises the test of well-founded conviction is unknown to them. They pick and choose as
they go through life, and are content to believe that
they possess the much-desired integrity because they
do not commit a major sin. This is self-deception at
its worst. The man who possesses integrity is a being
quite different from this. He has gained, either from
instinct by habit, or through training, the power to
think clearly, and he persists in asking of each new
problem what solution is prescribed for it by the principles that he holds. He is not swept off his feet by
the popular cry of the moment, for he knows that in
the life of man one popular cry succeeds another with
startling rapidity, and that all alike are apt to be quite
meaningless and misleading. Nor is he unduly cast
down because just now some policy in which he believes
appears to work badly and to disappoint those who
have most urgently pressed it forward. He knows
that in the long run worth asserts itself, and that so
long as history has a story to tell it has been the story
of constant improvement in man's conditions, of increasing control by man over his environment, and of

new and complicated adjustments between man and that environment as both become more complex in their natures and as they touch each other at more points.

I beg of you, as you go out from this university, to set your hearts upon intellectual as well as upon moral integrity, seeking a unity, a wholeness, a soundness, a steadfastness, a straightforwardness, which, taken together, are integrity itself. Do not be deceived with frauds and shams, and do not be alarmed with clamors and with cries. Remember well the lessons you have learned from nature; remember well the lessons you have learned from history; remember well the lessons you have learned from association with your fellows and from observation of them; and out of these lessons make each for himself a foundation of indestructible convictions upon which to build an intellectual life of increasing activity and value, not only to yourselves, but to your kind.

XXXIII

INTELLECTUAL CHARITY

Address on Commencement Day, June 1, 1910

INTELLECTUAL CHARITY

In the veritable babel of confusion which surrounds us on every hand, one is tempted to turn into a sermon on charity an address, however brief, to those who are to-day leaving their university behind them.

All forms of thought, as well as all forms of social and political life, are just now undergoing disturbance, upheaval, reconstruction. There are those who interpret these happenings and changes in terms of a new Renaissance, out of which are to come greater achievements of human intelligence and human character than the world has yet seen. There are others who prefer to think that we are living in a period of decadence and they find in the history of the decline and fall of the Roman Empire an analogy to what is going on round about us to-day.

It is more cheerful at least, and probably more correct, to take the brighter rather than the darker view of contemporary history. But whatever view be taken there is abundant room for the exercise of charity and abundant demand for it.

The air is filled with recriminations. On every hand motives are impugned, established standards are attacked, and proposals, however carefully studied, are torn to pieces by adverse and complaining critics before there is time to consider them fairly. There is hot applause for the loudest voice that makes the lowest appeal, and there is a readiness to believe ill of men and institutions which is not pleasant to witness. Particularly are those who represent the established order and those who have reached positions of prominence and power, however well deserved, made the objects of attack and the butt of complacent ridicule. These may not reply in kind, and, therefore, to that extent the popular demand for vigorous and even embittered controversy is disappointed. Those who have felt the helping hand of college and of university should go out into the world thus occupied and thus interested, with the fullest possible measure of intellectual charity. The human mind has a myriad facets, and it rarely reflects experience and observation in more than one of them. It takes the sum total of many individual pictures to tell the whole story of what actually happens. There is always room for the other point of view, and the occasions are rare indeed when there is not something to be said on the other side of any question.

Systematic training has for one of its main purposes the giving of a poise or balance that is to keep men and women from merely sharing, like dumb driven cattle, in the stampede of the moment. To the trained and disciplined minds of college and university graduates, evidence, as distinguished from assertion, ought to make a conclusive appeal.

Science, however, does not appear to be able to produce of itself fair and open mindedness, nor does literature or law; a subtle something which may perhaps be called intellectual charity must be added if into disputed questions there is to be carried not only the knowledge but the temperament which resolves difficulties and composes misunderstandings.

It is unbecoming for one whose mind has been trained by college and university discipline to become the mere partisan promoter of any person or cause. Enthusiasm he should have in fullest measure, but not the narrowness approaching bigotry which prevents his seeing the other side and appreciating a different point of view.

It must be the observation of every one that mankind is in a complaining mood. Ten meetings of protest are held for one meeting of approval; ten journalistic reproaches will be found for every journalistic commendation. In part, this attitude of mind and speech is due to superabundant egotism, but in larger part to lack of intellectual charity. The superabundant egotist does not like that which he cannot understand and cannot manage. His favorite mode of expression is the jeer or the sneer, and unfortunately he finds altogether too many amused listeners. Then, too, there is an odd gap or chasm between what many men profess to believe, between the principles which they profess to hold, and what they habitually do and say. This want of unity and harmony between profession and practice is a constant source of surprise and astonishment.

The fact probably is that mankind has not yet become accustomed to its new responsibilities. De-

pendence was converted into independence with surprising speed during the centuries from the sixteenth
to the nineteenth, and thereby a heavier load was
put upon humanity than it had yet been trained to
bear. Self-government, whether it be of the individual or of the community, remains after all these
long years a problem full of perplexity and difficulty.
Those of us who believe that mankind is steadily
climbing up-hill believe that all the forces in the world
which make for progress are preparing men for the
better discharge of responsibility and for the more
generous use of opportunity. We cannot deny, however—we dare not—that there is a long road yet to
travel.

It is just for this reason that the greater exercise
of intellectual charity is so sorely needed. Ignorance
is not perhaps itself a vice, but it is the mother of
many vices, and that partial ignorance which masquer-
ades as knowledge is a fruitful parent of everything
that ought not to be.

Carry out into the round of daily life an intellectual
charity. Do not insist upon imposing your own view
upon a universe that is itself larger and more complicated than any view which an individual, however
talented, can possibly hold. Try to understand that
others are as sincere and of as high motives as yours,
even though they appear to be moving in a quite
different direction.

If the colleges and universities cannot produce men
and women who will exercise intellectual charity, and

so soften the asperities and limit the controversies of which life is already too full, then where indeed shall intellectual charity be found?

There are many things to reflect upon on a day like this, but perhaps nothing is more worthy of our reflection on this day than those traits and characteristics which will help to shape the ordinary happenings of daily life by the high influences that go out from this university.

XXXIV

THE AGE OF IRRATIONALISM

Address on Commencement Day, June 7, 1911

THE AGE OF IRRATIONALISM

It is the fashion of historians and students of history to fasten a particular century, or age, or epoch, both in the imagination and in the memory by giving to it a name. We know what is meant when one speaks of the age of Pericles, or the age of chivalry, or the age of reason, as in each case mankind has hit upon a great personality, a distinctive institution, or an intellectual movement to serve at once as label and as guide-post. What shall we call the time in which we live, and how shall we designate the intellectual movement in which this great company of men and women has been trained to take, I hope and believe, an effective and an improving part?

This age of ours has been called the age of irrationalism. It is accused of oversubtlety and of preciosity, of impertinent self-confidence and of vulgar lack of respect for what has been. Irrationalism in one shape or another is said to furnish the dominant note for every department of our life, and to be as powerful in philosophy and in sociology as in literature. We are accused of having departed, and of seeking to depart still farther, from the approved ways and from established standards, and of having a feverish desire to find new things to say and new ways of saying them.

There is a good measure of truth in all this, and it is well to be on the lookout for the temptations and the dangers which our critics point out. It may well be that we have confounded novelty with originality and change with development, and that, like the ancient Athenians, we spend our time in nothing else but either to tell or to hear some new thing.

Certain it is that we are curiously under the influence of phrases, and that argument by epithet has come to take a high place in our ratiocination. To call a man, a movement, or a proposal by either a flattering or an obnoxious name is to remove them at once from the serious and thoughtful criticism of a large part of the population. Most persons are for or against a proposal because of what it has been called. This, of course, is not intelligent and it is not rational; but it is very common. So far as the larger public is concerned, the last half-century of science, a truly marvellous period, has made absolutely no impression on the thinking habit. It has destroyed many prepossessions and not a few beliefs, but it has not taught mankind to think. Our age is less reflective by far than was the eighteenth century or the first half of the nineteenth. Men are now so busy hunting for something new that they have no time to inquire what the word new means.

It is odd that we should have fallen so largely into this mood within a short generation after the doctrine of evolution had taken firm hold of the minds of cultivated men. If there is any one thing which that doctrine teaches more clearly and more insistently than another, it is that all true development and progress are out of and because of what has gone before, and that they are to preserve, not to destroy, those structures, habits, tendencies, and accomplishments which have shown themselves physically or morally fit; that is, suitable or worthy. It is not easy to explain why the condition which surrounds us exists, but exist it certainly does; and the educated man or woman of to-day has literally to struggle against being swept into the current of irrationalism.

Not long since there was a significant and amusing discussion in France as to why so large a proportion of the public men of that country come from one section. Many opinions were expressed, but one well-known social philosopher wrote that in his judgment the explanation was very simple. This, he said, is the age of the crowd and of the demagogue; that particular section of France provides both. Without either accepting this judgment or dissenting from it, we may be instructed by it. Whatever else this age may be, it certainly is the age of the crowd and of the demagogue. The crowd with its well-marked mental and moral peculiarities is everywhere in evidence; and demagogues political, demagogues literary, and demagogues religious din our ears with hungry cries. A torrent of talk is abroad in the land. The crowd just now, the world over, sways from right to left in policy, in belief, and in action, and cries out with wild enthusiasm to-day for the demagogue—political, literary, or religious—that it tramples under foot to-morrow. The art of being a demagogue appears to be easy and quick to learn, and the rewards of the successful practice of the art have strange fascination for minds and characters that one would like to think in all respects worthy. But we are under no obligation either to run with the crowd or to follow every demagogue.

The obvious attitude of the trained mind is not one of acquiescence in the temporarily popular or in the pursuit of the new, but one of searching for those basic principles revealed in the structure of human society and of nature, on which alone lasting policies and institutions can be built. To the man who does not think and who cannot think, the most reactionary proposal, if only it bear the label progressive, attracts as though it were a genuine advance. Selfishness and ambition clothed in the apparatus and nomenclature of virtue have great success in securing the support of those really disinterested and well-meaning persons for whom a label acts as an effective substitute for thought. We should not let them deceive or mislead us.

It is, of course, not easy to think. Very few human beings have formed the habit of persistent thinking in regard to those matters which press upon their attention and which solicit their interest and their help. Most of us are dominated by the newspaper head-line, and the men who write these head-lines are the real makers of current history.

In order to think and to form the habit of thinking,

one must have a point of departure. That point of departure may safely be taken in deep-rooted respect for what has been, for what has lasted, for what has charmed and delighted generation after generation and century after century. No one can intelligently face forward who has never looked intelligently back.

The true and most useful type of conservative is one who, as was said of King Alfred, bases his character upon old facts, but who accepts new facts as a reason for things. Change through conviction is real intellectual progress. Change through vague yearnings, through nervous excitement, through following a purveyor of phrases and platitudes, through rebellion against the laws of nature and of man, or through restless inability to understand, is not progress, but reaction. The typical self-styled progressive of to-day appears to believe that any leap in the dark is better than standing still. So he invents novelties in politics, in literature, and in religion, and plays with them in full view of a delighted and admiring public. This is irrationalism in full operation.

University study should have taught each of you that one of our main businesses in life is to form the habit of tracing facts, theories, projects, and schemes back to controlling principles, as well as to gain that genuine historical point of view which makes the words development and progress aglow with lively meaning.

These habits will defend us from the allurements of irrationalism, and will aid in defeating and destroying it. The power of robust and independent thinking is irrationalism's mortal enemy.

If those who go out from the universities are not proof against irrationalism, what hope is there for the less fortunate and the less advantaged ? One who, despite his training, feels a temptation to yield to irrationalism because it is popular and easy, may perhaps take a hint from Doctor Johnson. "I am sometimes troubled," said Boswell, "by a disposition to stinginess." "So am I," replied Johnson, "but I do not tell it."

XXXV

SUCCESS

Address on Commencement Day, June 5, 1912

SUCCESS

Another great army of men and women, filled, I am sure, with ambition and with hope, is about to march out through the gates of this university. Years of preparation, in some cases general, in others highly special and particular, lie behind. What does the future hold? Whither are we tending, what use, what application, are we to make of it all? One word springs almost inevitably to the lips of ardent youth: "My one wish is to be successful." When life's race is run and the account is made up once for all, everything will be found to hang upon the meaning of this word "success." As each individual interprets the object of his ambition, so will he mould his character. As each individual moulds his character, so will he leave a good or an evil repute behind, or pass through life unnoticed and unmarked.

"Success," said the poet Æschylus, "is man's god." What seers, what diviners of human nature and of its everlasting forms those ancient Greeks were! Truly success is man's god, and modern man worships that god far more devotedly and far more whole-heartedly than he worships Deity itself. Everything turns then on whether success is interpreted in terms of disciplined character, of generous service, and of real accomplishment, or whether it is measured in the base coin of greed, of passing popularity, or of the glamour of position which, like a rocket, only bursts into brightness to die in the dark.

A man's attitude toward success and his interpretation of it may easily change with his environment. In an age of predominant interest in letters and in art, a Dante and a Michael Angelo are successful, as are a Shakspere and a Rembrandt. In an age of discovery and of invention, the pendulum of attention swings to the philosophers and the men of science who blaze the way for new paths. In an age of commerce and of industry, requiring for their prosecution all the resources of huge amassments of capital, human interest passes to those who are the possessors of the greatest accumulations. The successful man of one age may in another be a mendicant even for reputation and for honor.

Man's chief responsibility is not for external things of any sort. It is for his inner self, for his standards, and his attitude to those many enticing things that lie without. Conduct is the one sure test of character, and success is only to be judged in terms of conduct. When the great ship *Titanic*, a veritable Vanity Fair, went staggering to its awful doom, merchant prince and pauper were alike stripped of their acquisitions and were left standing side by side as human souls to face death clad only in their characters.

Surely the world is old enough and man's experience is long and wide and deep enough to make all this unforgetable. Yet how constantly it is forgotten! On every hand we see men's characters offered for sale at the price of a paltry and passing gain. One sells his character for dollars; another for the soothing shouts of the populace; another for position and power, which, however high, are dishonored by the fact of their purchase at the cost of even a single human virtue.

That character which guides conduct to true success is a disciplined character. It is not fitful, or wayward, or blown about by every wind of doctrine, or moved by every change of circumstance. Discipline involves standards. The application of standards implies rules. A disciplined character, therefore, is a character which has fixed standards leading to definite rules of conduct. Unless life and study in a university have taught this lesson, the university has failed in its high purpose. The pressure for training to enable one to earn a living is all well enough in its way, but those who have not learned how to live will be of no benefit to civilization and of little value to themselves simply because they have learned how to make a living.

We need in our individual lives, and we sadly need in our national and international life, sobriety, stability, dignity of mind and of conduct. Of much that we see about us on every hand we must say, as Junius wrote to the Duke of Grafton: "I do not give you to posterity as a pattern to imitate, but as an example to deter."

When we are told that to resist some strongly urged movement is unpopular; that to hold fast to some principle which all human experience testifies to as

sound is to be behind the times; or that to fail to
join in the shouts of some gathered multitude is to
cut oneself off from influence and from power—a bid
is being made for our characters. It is being assumed
that they are for sale and that enough of these coins
will buy them. Unfortunately, in too many cases
that assumption is justified. Very many men, un-
happily, are not able to withstand the temptation of
immediate advantage. Their characters are undisciplined. Whatever may be their professions they have
no real principles. They are without standards to
which in time of doubt they resort for guidance and
for the measurement of conduct. No university can
justify itself if it goes on multiplying the number of
such as these. It can only be justified if, under its
influence, under its inspiration, and under its guidance,
learning is crystallized into wisdom and character is
built upon a sure foundation. When, as Seneca puts
it, "successful and fortunate crime is called virtue,"
we are a long way from any lasting civilization.

We are yet at school, all of us; and we are but
beginners at the great task of learning how to be men
and women. Good animals, useful animals, many of
us are; but the world stands sadly in need of real men
and women, of which there are all too few. I mean
men and women whose judgment is cautious but firm;
whose intelligence is quick but sound; and whose
characters are gracious but stable. It is only by the
making of men and women such as these that our
university shall be justified of its children.

XXXVI

THOROUGHNESS

Address on Commencement Day, June 4, 1913

THOROUGHNESS

Once more the gates of the university swing outward that these hundreds of young men and women may go forth into what is euphemistically styled the world. They carry with them, we all hope, happy and welcome memories of their life at Columbia, as well as no small burden of treasure that has been laid up while here. In that burden of treasure it is important that what Tennyson has called the thorough-edged intellect be found.

Thoroughness grows more necessary as it becomes less fashionable. Sound and disciplined thinking is hard to sustain in an atmosphere filled with the snapping sparks of rapidly following emotional outbursts. The patient examination of evidence is not easy at a time when trial by newspaper elbows to one side the slower process of trial by jury. The careful study of all that is involved in a proposal for some new sort of action in morals, in politics, or in society, is at a disadvantage when public attention is dragged quickly from one point of the emotional compass to another, and when masses of men, intent only on what they wish to get away from, have no sort of care for what they are going toward. Just now gossip displaces conversation; vice and loathsome disease are extolled as worthy of discussion in the drawing-room and of presentation on the stage; absorption in current topics (which to-morrow may be neither current nor topics) leaves no place for the genuine study of that history and that literature which have withstood Horace's *fuga temporum*. Every ruling tendency is to make life a Flat-land, an affair of two dimensions, with no depth, no background, no permanent roots.

For all this there is no support to be found in the study of science, of history, of literature, or of philosophy; least of all, in the lessons taught by the majestic doctrine of evolution. Each and all of these insists unendingly on thoroughness and on standards of excellence. There can be no doubt, however, that we moderns have lost much of the old respect for thoroughness. We seem to think that superficial brilliancy counts for more.

It is of vital importance for those who are just now forming their habits of mind and of conduct, and who are making for themselves a view of the world, to ponder all this and to realize what it means. He would be a poor scientist indeed who should describe the ocean in terms of its superficial currents, its calms, its storms, and its tempests only. The dark, silent depths, with their rich remains of ages that are past and with forms of life all their own, exerting as they do a profound influence on the habitable globe, would count for nothing in such a judgment. Or he would, likewise, be a poor scientist who should describe the earth's envelope in terms of the air which man breathes at or near the surface of the earth. The stupendous problems of physics, of chemistry, of mechanics, of astronomy, that grow out of and are illuminated by the characteristics of the upper atmosphere and of the ether, would go unnoted. In similar fashion the estimation of man's individual and social conduct in terms of his swiftly succeeding emotions fails to take account of the fundamental facts and laws that grow out of the nature of intellect and the necessities of character. Present feeling is by no means all that there is of life, although too often many are persuaded that it is so. The making of civilization is a gigantic task upon which the past, the present, and the future are all engaged, and in which the past, the present, and the future all have an interest, out of which interests grow rights. The observer of the surface of life, the impressionist, does not get an understanding of things as they are, but only of things as they at the moment appear to be.

If this university has not taught to every graduate to whom it offers to-day the hand of fellowship the lasting lesson of thoroughness, it has in so far failed no matter what else it may have done for him. He who has schooled himself to go to the bottom of things, to follow up every hint, and to pursue to its end each implication, has begun to get a true notion of the interdependence of nature and of life. In this way he learns the lesson that beneath superficial differences lie hidden, yet controlling, likenesses and unities. He comes to understand that however diffused the light of experience may seem to be, in reality it comes from a single source. He catches sight of the significance of principles, rules, laws, and he finds out how these principles, rules, laws manifest themselves in various and diverse ways that are a part of their life but not all of it.

The thorough-edged intellect is one that has learned these lessons and that has formed the habit of acting upon them. It is not satisfied with assertion demanding to be accepted as proof; with desire urging that it be identified with need; or with tumultuous clamor claiming to usurp the place of sober and reflective public opinion. It asks for reasons, it seeks for controlling principles, and it knows how to set about getting them. It is my earnest hope that these lessons of thoroughness have been so well learned and so pondered that they will shape the life and conduct of each one of you, and thereby bring new strength and new satisfaction both to yourselves and to the communities that you will serve.

XXXVII

LIBERTY

Address on Commencement Day, June 3, 1914

LIBERTY

It is a matter of no small concern to those who leave this university to-day for the purpose of entering upon the active work of life to realize what ideas and purposes are just now dominant in the minds of men and how these differ from those that have gone before. In the evolution of human ideas a curious cycle is observable. Beliefs and tendencies that have once appeared and that have been rejected or outgrown tend to reappear, sometimes in a new guise, with all the freshness of youth, and they are then acclaimed by those unfamiliar with their history as symbols of an advancing civilization. Probably the greatest waste recorded anywhere in human history is that which results from the attempt to do over again what has once been done and found disappointing or harmful. If the study of history were more real and more vital than it is ordinarily made, and if it showed ideas, tendencies, and institutions in their unfolding and orderly development, and if the lessons of history so studied were really learned and hearkened to, the world would be saved an almost infinite amount of loss, of suffering, and of discouragement.

When this college was young, the word that rose oftenest and instinctively to the lips was liberty. Men were then everywhere seeking for ways and means to throw off trammels which had been placed upon them by institutions of long standing but which were found to hamper them at every turn and to hem them in on every side. Liberty in those days meant not one thing, but many things. It meant freedom of conscience, of speech, and of the press; it meant participation in the acts of government and in the choice of governing agents; it meant freedom to move about over the world, to seek one's own fortune under strange skies and in foreign lands, there to live the life that one's own mind and conscience selected as most suitable. Liberty was then the watchword, not in the new world alone by any means, but in the old world as well and particularly in France, which has so often pointed the way of advance in the march of ideas. Standing in his place in the Convention during the fateful spring of 1793, Robespierre pronounced this definition of liberty which is almost the best of its kind: "Liberty is the power which of right belongs to every man to use all his faculties as he may choose. Its rule is justice; its limits are the rights of others; its principles are drawn from Nature itself; its protector is the law." Whatever judgment may be passed upon Robespierre's conduct, certainly his thought on this fundamental question of liberty was clear and sound.

But during the years that have passed we have moved far away from this view of what is important in life. There has grown up, not alone in America, but throughout the world, an astonishingly wide-spread belief in the value of regulation and restriction, not only as a substitute for liberty, but directly in opposition to it.   That against which the leaders of the race revolted a century and more ago is now pressed upon us in another form as a desirable end at which to aim. Not liberty, but regulation and restriction, are the watchwords of to-day, and they are made so in what is sincerely believed to be the greater public interest. John Stuart Mill, in his classic essay *On Liberty* saw and described these tendencies nearly fifty years ago, but even his clear vision did not foresee the length to which restrictions on liberty have now been carried.

Just as the driving force of an engine is to be found in the steam-chest and not in the brake, so the driving force in civilization will be found in liberty and not in restriction.   The cycle will, in due time and after a colossal waste of energy and of accomplishment, complete itself, and liberty will once more displace regulation and restriction as the dominant idea in the minds of men.   It is worth your while to take note, therefore, that while liberty is not now in the foreground of human thinking and human action, it cannot long be kept out of the place which of right and of necessity belongs to it.

The only logical and legitimate restriction upon liberty is that which is drawn from the like liberty of others.   That men may live together in family, in society, and in the state, liberty must be so self-disciplined and so self-controlled that it avoids even the appearance of license or of tyranny.

There are three possible ways of viewing and of

stating the relationship between the individual and the group or mass of which he forms a part.

In the first place, each individual may be regarded as an end in himself whose purposes are to be accomplished at all hazards and quite regardless of what happens to his fellows. This is that extreme form of individualism which has always ended, and must always end, in physical conflict, in cruel bloodshed, in violent anarchy, and in the triumph of brute force. It does not provide a soil in which ideas can flourish.

In the second place, each individual may be regarded as a mere nothing, a negligible quantity, while the group or mass, with its traditions, its beliefs, and its rituals, is exalted to the place of honor and almost of worship. The logical and necessary result of this view has always been, and must always be, from the standpoint of human accomplishment in institutions, stagnation, powerlessness, and failure. It is this view of life which has from time immemorial held so many of the great peoples of the Orient in its grip and which has set them in sharp contrast with the active and advancing life of the West for nearly two thousand years past.

The third view of the relationship of the individual man to the group or mass is the one that I would press upon you as offering the fullest measure of individual happiness and achievement and the greatest amount of public good. It stands between the philosophy of self-assertion, of disorder, of brute force, and of anarchy on the one hand, and the stagnation of an unprogressive civilization on the other. It is the view which emphasizes the individual to the utmost but which finds the conception of each individual's personality and accomplishment in his relations to his fellows and in his service to his kind. "He that loseth his life shall find it," is alike the last word of ethical philosophy and the supreme appeal to Christian morals. The enrichment and the development of the individual, in order not that he may acquire but that he may give; in order not that he may antagonize but that he may conciliate; in order not that he may overcome and trample under foot but that he may help and serve—this, as distinguished from the philosophy of disorder on the one hand and the philosophy of stagnation on the other—I call the constructive philosophy of the institutional life. It is built upon human individuality as a corner-stone and a foundation. The higher and loftier the structure rises, the more plainly it points upward, the heavier is the burden that the foundation bears, and the greater is its service to God and to man.

XXXVIII

THE OPEN MIND

Address on Commencement Day, June 2, 1915

THE OPEN MIND

In what spirit and in what attitude of mind the problems of practical life shall be approached by men and women who have had the benefit of the discipline and the instruction of a university are matters of grave concern to those charged with the university's oversight and direction. It is quite possible that one may be so assiduous in negligence and so skilful as to carry away from his college or university study little or nothing that will aid him to take a just, a sympathetic, and a helpful attitude toward the questions which life insistently asks. On the other hand, it is easily possible, and it should be normal and most usual, for the student to take with him from his college and university residence very much that will give him important advantage over his less fortunate fellows in estimating and in passing judgment upon men, upon tendencies, upon ideas, and upon human institutions. If he has gained from his study and discipline a mastery over method, a trained habit of withholding judgment until the evidence has been heard, a moral standard that knows instinctively the difference between right and wrong and that leads him to turn to the one as surely as it causes him to recoil from the other, then the university has furnished him well.

But granted the possession of these habits and traits, it is essential to beware of the closed mind.

The closed mind is not of itself conservative or radical, destructive or constructive; it is merely a mental attitude which may be any one of these or all of them in turn. By the closed mind I mean a mind which has a fixed formula with which to reach a quick and certain answer to every new question, and a mind for which all the great issues of life are settled once for all and their settlements organized into carefully ordered dogma. To the closed mind the world is a finished product and nothing remains but its interested contemplation. The closed mind may be jostled, but it cannot have experience. The name of a notable historic family, the house of Bourbon, has passed into familiar speech with the definition of one who forgets nothing and who learns nothing. The Bourbon typifies the closed mind.

There is another type of mind equally to be shunned. To be sure this type of mind is not closed, for, unfortunately, it is quite open at both ends. This is the type which remembers nothing and which learns nothing. To it the name of no historic family has yet been given. There is every prospect, however, that some contemporary name may, through constant association with this type of mind, yet become as distinguished and as familiar in the speech of our grandchildren as the name of the house of Bourbon is distinguished and familiar to us.

Open-mindedness is a trait greatly to be desired. It differs both from the closed mind and from the mind which consists wholly of openings. The open mind is ready to receive freely and fairly, and to estimate new facts, new ideas, new movements, new teachings, new tendencies; but while it receives these it also estimates them. It does not yield itself wholly to the new until it has assured itself that the new is also true. It does not reject that which is old and customary and usual until it is certain that it is also false or futile.

The power to estimate implies the existence of standards of worth and their application to the new experiences of the open mind. These standards are themselves the product of older and longer experiences than ours, and they form the subject-matter of the lesson which the whole past teaches the immediate present.

History offers a third dimension to the superficial area of knowledge that each individual acquires through his own experience. When one proclaims that he is not bound by any trammels of the past, he reveals the fact that he is both very young and very foolish. Such an one would, if he could, reduce himself to the intellectual level of the lower animals. He can only mean by such a declaration that he proposes to set out to discover and to explain the world of nature and of man on his own account and as if nothing had been done before him. He also jauntily assumes his own certain competence for this mighty and self-imposed task. His egotism is as magnificent as his wisdom is wanting. Such an one possesses neither an open mind nor a closed mind, but a mind open at both ends through which a stream of sensation and feeling will pour without leaving any more permanent conscious impression than the lapping waves leave on the sandy shore.

The man of open mind, on the contrary, while keenly alive to the experiences of the present, will eagerly search the records of the past for their lessons, in order that he may be spared from trying to do over again what has once been proved useless, wasteful, or wrong. The man of open mind will watch the rise and fall of nations; the struggle of human ambition, greed, and thirst for power; the loves and hates of men and women as these have affected the march of events; the migrations of peoples; the birth, development, and application of ideas; the records of human achievement in letters, in the arts, and in science; the speculations and the beliefs of man as to what lies beyond the horizon of sense, with a view to seeking a firm foundation for the fabric of his own knowledge and his own faith. His open-mindedness will manifest itself in hearkening to the testimony of other men, other peoples, and other ages, as well as in reflecting upon and weighing the evidence of his own short-lived and very limited senses.

There is a great difference between being intellectual and being intelligent. Not a few intellectual persons are quite unintelligent, and very many intelligent persons would hardly be classed as intellectual. One of the chief manifestations of intelligence is open-mindedness. The intelligent man is open-minded enough to see the point of view of those who do not agree with him and to enter in some measure into their feelings and convictions. He is able, also, to view the conflicting arguments and phenomena in proportion to each other and to rank the less significant of these below the more significant. It is quite possible to be intellectual and to manifest the closed mind; but it is not possible to do so and to be intelligent.

It is the constant aim of this college and university, by act and by precept, to hold up the value of open-mindedness and to train students in ways of intelligence. This university is the product of liberty, and it is passionately devoted to liberty. It finds in liberty the justification and the ground for open-mindedness, and also the source of those dangers which it is the business of the educated man to avoid. Open-mindedness in the university teaches the habit of open-mindedness in later life. Genuine open-mindedness guides to progress based upon wisdom. That each one of you may have caught something of this spirit and may constantly and effectively manifest it in the years to come is our earnest wish and hope.

XXXIX

THE KINGDOM OF LIGHT

Address on Commencement Day, June 7, 1916

THE KINGDOM OF LIGHT

It is our good fortune that there are in America men who do not permit the pressure of public service or of private business wholly to separate them from the intellectual life. About a quarter of a century ago, a group of such men made a visit to a farm near Phantom Lake in Wisconsin. The attraction of the lake proved so alluring and the occasion so enjoyable that the visit was repeated year after year. At each of these annual reunions some one of the company read a paper for the inspiration and to the delight of his associates. Some twenty years ago an eloquent and scholarly leader of the American bar, who was weighted heavily with professional responsibilities and who constantly rendered notable public service, took as the subject for one of these Phantom Club papers "The Kingdom of Light." The little-known essay which he then read is a priceless contribution to American literature. Like the almost equally unknown essay of John J. Ingalls on "The Blue Grass," it makes a sincere, a powerful, and a gracious expression of what is best and most natural in the thought of the unspoiled American.

The kingdom of light, as the writer of that paper described it, is an invisible commonwealth which outlives the storms of ages. It is a state whose armaments are thoughts, whose weapons are ideas, and whose trophies are the pages of the world's great masters. Toward this kingdom the steps of his associates were directed with subtly guiding thought and with singularly beautiful expression.

To-day a company of young men and young women, numbered by hundreds and almost by thousands, is about to march out from this great fortress of the mind and soul to undertake the invasion and the conquest of life. I beg of you in that march to turn your footsteps constantly and untiringly toward the kingdom of light. The world abounds in great cities, in broad plains, in rich mines, in ample opportunities for what we call personal and professional success; but all these are as Dead Sea fruit if we have not found our way, each one of us, into the kingdom of light. It is doubly hard just now to seek the protection and the seclusion of that kingdom. The world is roaring round about us; the noise and the darkness of a great tempest fills our ears and blinds our eyes. It needs patience, it needs courage, it needs real character, at such a time even to remember that there is a kingdom of light and that we wish to possess it.

Every possible excuse is always ready to offer itself for leaving undone those things that ought to be done. Lack of time, pressure of practical life, the needs of the moment, are all urged as reasons why we cannot make our way to the kingdom of light and enjoy it as we should like to do. After granting all that may be justly claimed for lack of time, after granting all that may be urged on behalf of the practical needs of the moment, it remains true that the man who allows his mental and spiritual nature to stagnate and to decay does not do so from lack of time or from the pressure of other things, but from lack of inclination. To enter into the kingdom of light, to live with great thoughts, to enjoy the beauty of letters and of art, to absorb the experience and to share the ambitions and the hopes of mankind, all this is primarily a matter of character and of will. The material obstacles that stand in the way of its accomplishment are too often sternly present, but they are far from insurmountable. Effort, persistent directed effort, will bring us quickly to the kingdom of light and keep us within its kindly governance.

The philosophers rule the world, and they have always ruled it since philosophy began. The man of action may not know whence his ruling ideas and purposes come; he may not even know what those ruling ideas and purposes are. Nevertheless, they are there and they are ruling. They may be the product of a good philosophy, or they may be the product of a bad philosophy; but of some philosophy they are certainly the product. Ideas direct conduct. He who has entered into the kingdom of light moves easily and in friendly converse among ideas. He chooses those that he would have guide him in his daily business. At nightfall, perhaps, he retires within the quiet boundaries of this kingdom to refresh himself anew by pondering, by weighing again those thoughts that console, and those thoughts that elevate.

There is no such thing as a common, a humdrum, or a sterile life, unless we make it so ourselves. "The rainbow and the rose," says my author, "will give their colors to all alike. The sense of beauty that is born in every soul pleads for permission to remain there." If we will but look for it, there is something ennobling and uplifting in every vocation to which a man can put his hand. Every activity of life has its material aspect and its spiritual aspect. It has its result in visible accomplishment and it also has its result in invisible mind-building, will-building, and intellectual enjoyment.

Just now we have been speaking much of a little town on the river Avon, a town which, compared with London, with Manchester, with Liverpool, is negligible in size; but we have been speaking of Stratford because the fortunes and the influence of letters are indissolubly linked with it. It is a capital city of the kingdom of light. It is not potent as are the cities of commerce and of capital and the homes of great populations; but when the rising tide of time has swept all these into the valley of forgetfulness the capital cities of the kingdom of light will remain safely seated upon their high hills.

It is into this kingdom that I would have each son and daughter of Columbia enter. Its gates are many and various, its high places are of different kinds and of different ages, but from them all one looks eastward to to-morrow's rising sun. The purpose of performance is to pave the way for new promise; the purpose in looking back is to fix the direction of the line that guides us in moving forward. If we can but learn the lessons that the kingdom of light has to teach, if we can but share the enjoyment and the elevation of spirit that the kingdom of light has to offer, we shall be made wise and strong for new accomplishment that will bring to man new comfort, new happiness, and new satisfaction.

In setting out upon this journey, you carry with you the blessing and the good-will of the university of your choice.

XL

A WORLD IN FERMENT

Address on Commencement Day, June 6, 1917

A WORLD IN FERMENT

The hundreds, indeed the thousands, of American youths who pass out from this university to-day go into a new and a strange world. It is more than a world at war; it is a world in ferment. From the steppes of Russia all the way across Europe and America and around to Japan and China men and nations are not only engaged in a titanic military struggle but they are also examining and, when necessary, quickly readjusting and reorganizing their customary habits of thought and of action, private as well as public. It is not easy, perhaps it is impossible, to find an Ariadne who will give us a guiding thread through this labyrinth of change. Presuppositions that have long sustained the solid fabric of personal and of national conduct have been destroyed. Assumptions that have seemed to be made certain by the earlier progress of man have disappeared under the pressure of the latest manifestations of trained human capacity for evil.

Before such a scene the timid will despair, while the reckless will affect an indifference that they cannot really feel. The wise will follow a different course. They will not be hurried into judging of normal man on the basis of his latest abnormalities, and they will not permit themselves to forget all that human history teaches because the happenings of the moment seem to teach something quite different. The wise will not lose their sense of proportion in judging of events in time, in space, or in circumstance.

Each individual whose training has really reached the depths of his nature, and so has formed his habits of thought and of action, will first examine his own relation to what is going on in the world, and will next inquire how that which is going on is to be judged in terms of everlasting standards of right and of wrong, of progress, and of decline. He will first of all find himself to be a member of a politically organized group which is a nation. He will find himself beholden to that group, to its traditions, to its ideals, and to its highest interests, not as a parasite but as a strengthening and a contributing force. Recognition of this relationship will be the basis of his loyalty, and the measure of his loyalty will be not lip-service but sacrifice. He will in this way discover that the ends of which his group or nation is in search are the ends that he must strive to accomplish. It will not be difficult for him to see that in most cases, in the vast majority of cases, these ends are to be reached by persuasion, by argument, by consent, but that in the last resort, if they be ends on which turns the whole future of mankind, they must, if need be, find protection and defense in physical and military force. This is a sad but significant evidence of the incomplete development of mankind.

He will next apply the standards of moral excellence and approval to the present-day conduct of men and of nations, with a view to determining whether the changes that are going forward are making for human progress or for human decline. He will be led to answer this question by the relative importance accorded to ideas and ideals. If men and nations are engaged in a blind struggle for material gain, for mere conquest, for revenge, or for future privileges, then what is going on is in high degree a manifestation of bestiality in man. If, on the other hand, the struggle be one for the establishment on the largest possible scale, in the securest possible way, of those institutions and opportunities which make man free, then the contest rises to the sublime. In this latter case every contestant on behalf of such a cause is a hero, and every one who offers his life and his strength and his substance is a sincere lover of his kind.

It may therefore well be that it is for the issue of this war to determine whether mankind is still in progress or has begun his decline. If the moral, the economic, and the physical power of men and of nations that love freedom is adequate to its establishment on a secure basis, then mankind is still in progress and new vistas of satisfaction and of accomplishment are to be spread out before him. If, on the other hand, the strength of men and of nations that love freedom is not adequate to this severe task, then man has crossed the Great Divide of his political history and is to begin a descent into those dark places where force and cruelty and despotism wreak their will. Nothing less than this is the alternative which now confronts not alone the nations of the earth, but every individual in each one of those nations. The responsibility for action and for service cannot be devolved upon some one else, least of all can it be devolved upon government officials and government agencies. These have their great part to play, but in last resort the issue will be decided, not by governments, not even by armies and by navies, but by men and women who are the support of all these and whose convictions and stern action are the foundation upon which government and armies and navies rest.

Let there be no faltering by any son or daughter of Columbia. The clock time is about to strike the most portentous hour in all history. May each child of this ancient university take inspiration and courage from Alma Mater herself, who in her long life has in time of trouble never wavered, in time of danger never hesitated, in time of difficulty never doubted. May all her children be forever worthy of her!

XLI
NEW VALUES

Address on Commencement Day, June 5, 1918

NEW VALUES

The university which assembles to-day to mark the passing of another year is sadly depleted in numbers. Nearly 350 officers of administration and instruction have put aside their academic duties in order to enter the military or naval service of the United States or to take part in some other public work essential to winning the war. Our roll of students has fallen from more than 22,800 to less than 19,500, and each week sees new groups of both men and women turning from their tasks here to accept some form of public service. We would not have it otherwise. The greater the university's sacrifice, the greater the university's service. The spirit of 1776 and the spirit of 1861 are fortunately no less potent here in this twentieth century than when they first found expression. The loyal devotion of Columbia University and its zeal for service are to-day writing a new and proud chapter of our academic history.

What can be said to those who remain to take part in these commencement exercises that has not already been said an hundred times and in an hundred ways?

The world now understands the issue with which it is faced, and to none is it probably more clear and definite than to those who are this day to close the period of their formal academic study. But we must take note that amid all the evils and horrors and outrages of this war there are to be seen a few fortunate accidents. Whole nations find themselves exalted to new and lofty planes of noble feeling and of generous emulation in sacrifice. Myriads of men and women count as nothing the luxuries and comforts upon which they had grown to depend, in order that they may find some post of public usefulness and devotion. The universal ambition is to be as near the firing-line as possible. These facts indicate that the rude shock of war has been effective to establish a new scale of values. Material gain, great authority, noteworthy power, comfortable ease, have all been cast aside for something that is found to be more valuable still.

The heart of man has made an articulate cry, and the world has heard it! It is a cry for those fundamental things that lie at the very foundation of a reasonable and a moral life. It is a cry for the protection of the weak against the strong. It is a cry for the enforcement of human law and for the establishment of human justice. It is a cry for the protection of a nation's plighted word against those who would treat it, when convenience demands, as only a scrap of paper! It is a cry for freedom, for liberty, for opportunity to live a life of one's own choice and making, provided only that every other man's equal right be not restricted thereby. For these things men and nations are ready to sacrifice all that they possess, and to kill their fellow men whom they have not seen and whom they do not know, in order that of these things they may not be deprived.

Nations do not go to war over the multiplication table, or the Julian calendar, or the metric system, or the precise day and hour at which a total eclipse of the sun takes place. All of these matters are highly important to the conduct and disposition of civilized life and to the convenience of man; but no one of them, not ten thousand other facts like them, grip men's souls and stir their spirits as does the slightest happening that marks a wrongful infringement of human liberty, or a wrongful denial of human opportunity.

The reason why men and nations fight for these things which some still think comparatively trivial, but which so powerfully affect human life and human aspiration, is that they are measured by a scale of values all their own, and with which no mere material event can possibly compare.

We have heard much of efficiency, of training for some specific place or function in human society; but the whole world now understands that efficiency is without moral quality, and may become a mere instrument to most immoral and destructive ends. Efficiency may temporarily exalt a nation, but it cannot save it from that destruction which efficiency, when apart from high human purpose and lofty ideals, certainly carries in its hand.

This is one of the great lessons of the war. It is a lesson which should be quickly applied to correct some of the rather shabby and superficial doctrines that are all round about us as to the purpose and methods of education. These may be based upon efficiency, they may include and attain efficiency, and yet be quite below that plane of excellence upon which modern man wishes and intends to move.

The higher levels of activity and devotion are the ones which the war has revealed to us as making the strongest appeal to civilized man. It is at these levels we shall wish to walk; and it is at these levels that we shall wish our nation, and those splendid peoples at whose side she stands, to reconstruct the world for a new era of progress, of happiness, and of established international peace.

The call of the coming future is powerful beyond all compare. The joy of living, when there is so much to do, should spur on in unexampled fashion those who are to become leaders of the next generation, for these are to be charged with almost incredible responsibility for guiding the world in search of its new accomplishments and its new purposes. All knowledge, all training, all capacity are now being consecrated to this great aim.

It is the profound conviction of the university you this day leave, but to whose membership you will always belong, that you understand these new values and that they will guide your lives.

XLII

DISCIPLINE

Address on Commencement Day, June 4, 1919

DISCIPLINE

For a long time to come the world will be staggering under the blows inflicted by the war upon its political, its economic, and its social systems. For a still longer time the world will be learning the lessons of the war's experience and interpreting anew, in the light of that experience, not only its aims and ideals but its methods of life and work.

The two million Americans, drawn from every walk of life, who went to France to offer their lives if need be in the high cause of international justice and political liberty are coming back with new and broader outlook, with deeper convictions, and with a sterner sense of the realities of life. In less degree, perhaps, these same lessons have been learned by those soldiers and sailors who remained at home, and by the tens of millions of men and women who followed with anxious solicitude the events of each succeeding day in the war's history.

Unless all signs fail, the war has taught a new respect for discipline and has re-established in the minds of men some ancient convictions that had lately shown signs of weakening. It was, for example, the exceptionally effective and minutely organized discipline of the German people, political, economic, and social, as well as military, that made the war an actual fact. It was the lack of an equally effective and well-ordered discipline on the part of the people of the allied nations that permitted the issue to hang so long in the balance. Amazing courage, limitless sacrifice, and unbreakable wills sustained the shock of battle against overwhelming odds until that full organization of national power and competence which discipline aims to effect had been brought into existence. When that happened, the war was speedily won, for the self-imposed discipline of the free peoples was certain to be immensely superior to the arbitrarily imposed discipline, even though cheerfully assented to, of the Germans.

In similar fashion, thousands and tens of thousands of individuals whose lives had been running at loose ends and who had never had the occasion or the invitation to summon all their resources for the accomplishment of some high and definite purpose found, sometimes to their surprise, that there was a specific and helpful place for them in the closely organized military or economic life of the nation. To hold this place one condition was absolutely necessary; namely, that they accept discipline and obey orders. In a twinkling of an eye these men, young and old, found themselves working cheerfully and unselfishly as parts of a great effective engine of national expression. Much in the way of achievement that had seemed beyond their reach was now of every-day occurrence. Life was filled with new satisfactions because there was a steadily deepening consciousness of work that was worth while being worthily done. The unrest and the dissatisfaction which so many of these brave youths feel to-day is due in no small measure to the fact that after this striking experience, with its revelation of their own value to the world, they are sent back on briefest warning to a life in which their part and place are by no means so definite or so clearly defined, and in which they see disorganization and wastefulness seeming to usurp the place of discipline and that precise adaptation of means to ends with which they had become familiar.

These contrasts afford material for grave reflection. Through long centuries of observation and experience mankind had learned very much about the meaning and the methods of discipline, but in the decade or two immediately preceding the war there had been a steadily growing tendency to overlook all this and to assert either that general discipline was impossible or that it was unimportant. The war has rudely overturned a good many tables of irrelevant statistics and has made it unnecessary longer to pay attention to elaborate records of unmeaning experiments. The hard sense of men again asserts itself and points clearly to discipline as a necessary element in individual, in social, and in national progress. All depends on the use which is made of discipline and on the purposes which a disciplined individual, a disciplined society, or a disciplined nation aims to accomplish.

The beginnings of discipline are found in man's contact with the forces of nature. He soon learns that he is limited by the instruments and the material which nature provides, by the processes which we call nature's laws, and by his own general relation to an environment which, however much it may submit itself to inquiry and to modified control, stubbornly resists being done away with entirely.

The second step in the development of discipline is the experience of the race and the teachings of our elders. These save us from the necessity of having to make over again the costly and painful mistakes of those who have gone before us. They tell us in unmistakable terms that certain courses of action and certain habits are advantageous and are to be followed and built up, while certain other courses of action and certain other habits are disadvantageous and are to be let alone. A very large part of formal education consists in learning these lessons of human experience and in coming gradually to understand the reasons for them.

The third and final step in discipline is when the individual of maturing powers takes immediate control of his own life, and by his own will and because of his own understanding imposes upon himself the limitations and restrictions which human experience teaches to be necessary or expedient. The aim of all discipline, therefore, is self-discipline. We study the limitations which nature imposes upon man and we learn the lessons which past experience teaches, in order that man may govern himself in the light of these, and constantly advance through a progress that is constructive because it is built upon the sure foundation of a knowledge of nature and a knowledge of human happenings.

The notion that men may drift through life without discipline or without purposed shaping of their conduct and yet be worthy of human opportunity and human aspiration is not very complimentary to mankind, or even to the lower animals. The instincts of the latter provide them with the protection against disaster which discipline and self-discipline offer to man. Drifting through life, whether it be a life of comparative ease or a life of comparative hardship, is not a worthy use of personality. The period of study and formal preparation is the period when youth are absorbing from nature and from human experience the raw material with which to construct their own life-aims and their own course of ordered conduct. If school and college and university training and teaching do not supply these, they have sadly failed. Information is no substitute for discipline, nor will mere skill or competence take its place. Information is useful if it be the material for reflection, but otherwise it has only the value of an index to an encyclopædia. Skill and competence are useful if they are organized for the accomplishment of a fine and clearly understood purpose. Otherwise they easily become the instruments of vice and crime. It is man's purpose which is the key to his character, and it is man's self-discipline for the accomplishment of his purpose which is the explanation of his success or failure in life. And by success is not meant getting rich. The mere heaping up of great wealth, which a generation ago was thought to be a laudable occupation, is now felt to be a rather stupid use of time and opportunity. If wealth be gained and then used for human advancement, that is one thing; but if it be heaped up and merely left like a ball and chain around the feet of the next generation, that is quite another matter.

A self-disciplined nation made up of self-disciplined men and women, training its youth through discipline to self-discipline, is a nation that is building on a sure foundation not only for prosperity but for that happiness, that usefulness, and that satisfaction which give to prosperity its real significance. To aid in that accomplishment has been the aim and the purpose of Columbia University through a hundred and sixty-five years. May your memories of the days spent in Columbia's halls be ever bright and welcome, and may both success and satisfaction accompany you as you do your part in the work of the world.

XLIII

CAPTAINS OF A GREAT EFFORT

Address on Commencement Day, June 2, 1920

CAPTAINS OF A GREAT EFFORT

A world in ferment has passed into a world perplexed. Not since the invention of printing and the rise of the common school, with the consequent spread of knowledge among the people, have so huge and so little understood forces been at work in the world as is the case at this moment. We are standing, in a state of unstable equilibrium, at the summit of a vast upheaval out of the political, the social, and the economic life of the modern nations. This upheaval has long been under way. The discovery and the settlement of America were both a symptom and a cause. The struggle between parliament and the king and the overthrow of the Stuarts were both a symptom and a cause. The development of modern science, the philosophic and economic doctrines whose beginnings are associated with the eighteenth century, and the French Revolution itself, were both a symptom and a cause. The progress of invention, the development and the applications of steam and of electricity, the industrial revolution, the gathering of increasing units of population in large cities, the weakening and the decline of faith, first in the unseen and eternal and next in the power of fundamental principles of life and of morals, were both a symptom and a cause. If the Great War had not sprung from the lust of Teutonic Imperialism in 1914, it now seems, as we look back, not unlikely that it would have sprung from some other cause a few years later. The beast in man lies very near the surface and the worst side of human nature is constantly ready to challenge its best side to mortal combat.

In all these facts and happenings are to be found the ground for the world's perplexity. Its old standards of weight and measurement in matters political, in matters social, and in matters economic will no longer serve. To change the figure, the new wine of experience and of aspiration cannot be poured into the old bottles of tradition and convention. In consequence, the world is perplexed. It cannot—it feels that it must not—throw away the great achievement and rich experience of the past, and it has not yet learned how to apply these to the new conditions. Human nature is once again being subjected to a searching test of capacity before the stern tribunal of history. Those who have faith in mankind are serenely confident that, despite the troubled outlook, all will yet be well. Those who have lost faith in mankind see "not light, but rather darkness visible," and civilization on its way to final ruin.

If indeed these be times that try men's souls, then they are good times in which to live. None but the weakling or the poltroon will turn his back upon the tremendous struggle to put civilization upon a new and yet stouter foundation. The call to men and women of capacity, of courage, and of character is clarionlike in its clearness. It is not a call to revolu-

tion; it is a call to hasten evolution. It is a call to
summon all the resources of a nation—the resources
physical and material, the resources intellectual and
moral, the resources economic and political—for a
successful effort at reconstruction and advance, not
for ourselves alone but for the whole world of civilization. The old and tested principles are still sound and
true if they be stripped of the seaweed that has grown
upon them during their long voyage across the seas of
human experience. The old characteristics of clear
conviction, straight thinking, human sympathy, fine
feeling, rugged determination are the characteristics of
the conquerors and the builders of to-morrow. Do
not wait for others to move. Come up out of the
valley of despair, of hopelessness, and of impending
disaster, and help make the world better and stronger
yourself.

Our nation has passed through the shadow of a
great danger and has surmounted that danger by a
great effort which history will never fail to·recall with
gratitude. The danger was lest physical isolation and
a sense of separation from the world's troubles might
lead to indifference, to selfish materialism, and to that
sure decay which follows upon self-satisfied and effort-
less national contentment. Providence ruled otherwise. The heart of the American people was moved,
its soul was stirred, and its conscience was quickened
to lively action, by a rapid succession of events which
heralded the quick coming of the day of doom unless
the cause of human liberty was saved from the brutal

rule of organized force. The American people rose, men and women alike, by the million. Each state, each community, each household, contributed its effort, and the solemn spectacle of one hundred and ten millions of free men and free women, moving almost as one toward the accomplishment of a high and noble purpose, was offered to the world. That effort, so characteristic of an intelligent, high-minded, and liberty-loving people, had its captains. There were captains of those who bore arms and who went, life in hand, singing the songs of home and of country, to the front line of battle. There were captains of those who go down to the sea in ships, ceaselessly to keep watch amid darkness and storm and wave, lest harm happen to men and to those things which minister to the life of men. There were captains of those who bring succor and relief to the stricken, to the wounded, to the starving, whose ministry of mercy is so beautiful an accompaniment of that last form of high effort which calls for the sacrifice of human happiness and of human life. There were captains of those who minister to the minds and souls of armies and of navies, that, as the battle raged and as the angel of death hovered over them seeking and choosing whom to strike, their thoughts might be turned to "whatsoever things are true, whatsoever things are lovely, whatsoever things are just, whatsoever things are pure, whatsoever things are of good report." All honor to these many captains of the nation's many-sided effort; all highest honor to those captains of captains whose knowledge, whose skill, whose insight, whose foresight, and whose devotion brought victory in all its forms to the cause upon whose success the heart of the American people was so surely set.

Men and women of Columbia, those of you who to-day go out by the thousand to take hold of the task of life, go out from these historic doors at a great moment. You go out when the university has summoned to its presence the captains of the captains in the nation's great effort, that it may invite them to a high place in its notable membership and say before all the world, with sincerity, with full appreciation, and with grateful joy, that they have deserved well of their country; that they have added to its repute and renown, and that this ancient university wishes forever to associate its name with theirs and their names with Columbia.

XLIV

FAITH IN THE FUTURE

Address on Commencement Day, June 1, 1921

FAITH IN THE FUTURE

The active and ingenious mind of Professor Bergson has lately reaffirmed his belief that the future is not pre-existent in the present, and that events are not possible until they have happened. One may resist the temptation to embark on the sea of speculation to which this statement invites, and yet be stimulated by it to examine one's attitude toward the future and the effect of this attitude upon the conduct of his daily life. It is a mathematical truism that the present is wholly a creature of human imagination. Time is in persistent flow, and as the sound of the word present dies upon our ears that moment to which it refers is already past and another is fleetly following it. The future does not lie some distance ahead of us, only to be reached by long travail and over many obstacles. It strikes us in the face instantly as we open our eyes to view the world in which we live. The true fact is that faith in the future is the foundation, and pretty much the sole foundation, for all that we do and prepare to do. Education, for example, is toward a more or less definite end, and that end is always ahead of us. Work is undertaken for some set purpose, and that purpose is always ahead of us. Accumulation is sought for some hoped-for use, and that use is always ahead of us. Faith in the future is the only justification for human activity of any sort whatsoever.

The human race has had its full share of pessimists, philosophic and other, but only occasionally have these pessimists had the courage of their professed convictions and sought to avoid facing the future by their own tragic act. The majority of men are, to be sure, unreflecting, unconcerned with the future, and indifferent to it save as they instinctively take it for granted. Others, and among these should be all those who have caught the spirit of a true university, have faith in the future, and by that faith are led so to shape their acts and thoughts that the future as it comes shall be better than the present as it goes. This faith in the future is justified and in high degree helpful in the guidance of life if it rest on reasonableness and on a full understanding of the fact that what has been merges into what is and makes way for it.

It pleases some ardent and hopelessly youthful spirits to portray themselves as in revolt against things as they are; but this is not the constructive temper or the spirit in which to go about the serious business of making the world better. An appreciation of the present and an understanding of the past are a far better preparation for the improvement of the future than a dissatisfaction with the present and a contempt for the past can possibly be. Faith in the future includes faith in that upon which the future rests and out of which it must grow. Professor Bergson may be right in his view that the future is not preformed in the present, but surely he would not wish us to believe that the future stands in no relation to the present and is not in fact, if not in form, a product of forces, whether hidden or other, that are now at work in the hearts and minds of men.

Contentment is as lofty and fine a state of mind as smug satisfaction is unbecoming and unworthy. Faith in the future will make use of contentment, but it can do nothing with smug satisfaction. The man whose mind is closed to all proposals for change, for reasonable experiment with the unfamiliar and untested, is stubbornly without faith in the future. His mind and spirit move in a closed circle and are the captives of their present environment. The free spirit will use its environment as a stepping-stone to new enterprises, to new experiments, and to new undertakings. It will not be wasteful or extravagant of effort, because it will remember what past experience and past experiment have taught, and what enterprises and undertakings have been definitely set aside as unwise, unbecoming, or unworthy. As man goes forward in civilization, progresses, as we call it, his field of choice is steadily limited as possible courses of thought and action are shown to be stupid, or harmful, or wicked. Slowly through the centuries there emerge those choices from which selection must be made, and these become ideals by which to guide and to shape the conduct of men and of societies. Faith in the future means faith in those ideals which survive the test of rational experience and severe experiment.

It is said of Pythagoras that when asked what time was, he answered that "It is the soul of the world."

If time be the soul of the world, then the future is the material out of which the world's living body is to be built and by means of which its work is to be done. If to our limited human imagination the future is the yawning void which Marcus Aurelius thought it to be, then it is our task to fill that void full to the brim with worthy accomplishment. As this accomplishment grows in importance and in high quality from century to century and from age to age, it will join with those ideals which persist because of their nobility and their worth, to justify the deepest faith of man in

> "One God, one law, one element,
> And one far-off divine event
> To which the whole creation moves."

INDEX

INDEX